I0840830

PREFACE

In this book are the most viewed posts from the blog, frohmedporche@blogger.com. These posts gave a very interesting insights on some popular topics that range from politics, social issues, entertainment, sports, and fitness. There were readers who held similar beliefs to the views expressed in the posts while others stood firm with their viewpoints however, they were able to gain a new understanding of the topics by looking through a different lens from a different perspective with an open mind. A summation is included with every post to provide an update of the effect the topics had or continue to have on social life. This book marks the end of the blog but there will be a Volume II in the future of posts that readers found profound from the blog to complete the collection.

Table Of Contents

The Last Decade Of Rap Music
(Hip Hop You Will Stop)

An art form was introduced to radio in the late 70's and then spread throughout the United States over its airwaves expressing a new culture and views of an influential Black and Hispanic generation. It evolved and gained America's attention during the 80's and it became the top genre of music in the 90's. A music that started in the Black and Hispanic neighborhoods of New York City fascinated people of all ages, races, and sexual orientation during the 2000's. Its style and language would transcend the streets and capture the attention of college students and accepted by college professors who spoke the language in classes. This vernacular permeates through television, movies, and social media.

Rap music and hip hop culture has thrived for almost 40 years. Most of its original artists and people who shaped the culture are now grandparents. They are the roots that have made it possible for artists of today to blossom while others benefit from using the culture. However, those who were at the beginning of rap and hip hop are pointing out that the form of rap music today does not resemble the rap music they help create and advance in popularity. It has caused some of the older generation to be at odds with those of the younger generation about the state and direction of the music.

A realization for these lovers of hip hop is that rap music will eventually fade into the musical genre abyss. Classical, big band, ragtime, jazz, blues, rock, hard rock, disco, and funk at one time were prominent forms of music during certain eras but as their generations aged, enthusiasm for that style of music waned as the youth diluted the music or created a new form of music that appealed to their generation. It is a losing battle for the older generation to believe their form of rap music along with the hip hop culture can exist in its original form when the younger generation does not have the same love for the music and the culture has been corrupted. Youthful artists have been blinded by the illusion of making money and that being successful will sustain their genre of music but when fans lose interest in the music there will be no demand for it and younger music fans will move on to a new genre that appeals to their generation.

       After all of the profits have been made and rap music is no longer a viable source of revenue, very little money will be afforded the genre as the focus will be directed to finding the next profitable form of music. Rap music may continue on a underground level supported by die hard hip hop fans but this is possibly the last decade of rap being the most popular form of music. The energy, passion, and skill of its originators with intense support from the hip hop community is lacking in the rap music of today. In the beginning, there was an intent to spread the music and the culture but the modern day intent is to market the artist and build their brand while supporters of the music have become followers who accept less and never require more from their favorite rap artists. Rap music and hip hop has been spread so thin that it is hard to find any remnants of its true essence. It is the last of the ketchup in the bottom of the bottle that has been mixed with water to form an inferior product that has traces of the original but is void of the essentials that was used to create it.

Posted 11/16/2016

SUMMATION. While rap music is dominating the music charts, there are almost no rap artist ranking among the top grossing tours. Many popular and successful rap artists are having to cancel dates on their concert tour due to the lack of ticket sales. There will be speculation that fans are tiring from the bravado, misogyny, violence, and vulgarity in the music but in actuality, it is sub par music lacking in quality and the attitudes of the artists. The genre has been saturated with *"microwave hits"* and very few great albums while artists have the expectation that fans will accept any music they put out and buy tickets to their shows because of their popularity.

A strong undercurrent from a new sound is moving music lovers to give another genre some attention. Talented young artists are pushing rhythm and blues to the forefront with a feel of soul music that is resonating with many listeners. These artists have exceptional voices and some of them are musicians, all are attracting people to their shows with fabulous live performances. Hit songs from these artists are lasting more than a week with fans who find the lyrics of the songs refreshing with depth and meaning. As times change, so does the temperament of the people. There will always be people who are fans of rap music but it will be pushed aside as other great genres were in the past.

I Am Not Impressed With You Niggers (Niggas)
(No Matter How You Say It)

I am not impressed by you calling yourself a real nigga (nigger), a thug nigga (nigger), a gangsta nigga (nigger) to embellish yourself when you are actually degrading yourself. A more effective description of yourself would be a real man, dependable man, a strong Black man. Labeling yourself as a nigga (nigger) states to the world that you are a nigger (nigga) because you are using a demeaning moniker that was attached to Black people by their oppressors. It shows the oppressor's descendants that the program is still working and they do not have to reinforce it because Blacks continue the destructive behavior by using it on each other.

I am not impressed when you refer to your friend as *"my nigga (nigger)"* because now you are spreading the illness of your mind through language that is not only heard by the person your talking to but anyone who can hear the sound of your voice. A better greeting would be my friend, my brother, my honorable Black man. If you are not corrected by the person you are speaking to then the ignorance has become so pervasive that it has dulled their cognitive awareness of being insulted. This shows people who discriminate against Blacks that the program has become so powerful that it is unstoppable.

I am not impressed that you call your man *"my nigga (nigger)"* and he calls you *"my bitch"* because this shows a descension into a degenerative behavior that there may not be a possibility of recovery. Any children born from this union and grows up witnessing this behavior will possibly replicate it front of their children. This breathes another century of life into this demeaning slur that has spread just as kudzu has through the South with no signs of slowing down. It is true, that a system of laws have kept Blacks in a deprave condition but their soul-destroying practices have also contributed to them staying in that condition.

There are only weeks left in the last term for President Obama and the lid has been taken off this erosive epithet (nigger, nigga). It is being used more in music and movies, talk shows and the news, and by discontented voters during the campaign and after the election. Some Blacks believe in using the dissenting label to show unity and power but non-Blacks hear a slur that was used on the ancestors of Blacks and they have no problem on using it on modern day Blacks because Black people use it on each other. This slur has no limitations as it has been used on famous and professional Blacks just as much as it has been used on common and poor Blacks. President Obama has not been exempt as it touched the man in the highest executive office of the United States and leader of the free world.

Black youth in the 1990's explained their use of the epithet as a greeting between each other and showing unity with each other. They specifically brought attention to their different spelling of this despicable label to show their version of the epithet has a different meaning. Years later, White youth decided they wanted to use the derogative label and argued that if Blacks can use it then they should be able to say it, also. There was pushback by Blacks who referred to the slur in its original meaning. To this day, Blacks get upset with Whites who say it but remain silent when other Blacks say it. A dilemma that is easy to fix.

Stop saying it! There are no exemptions and

there are no different definitions. Berries, leaves, and twigs can be put on excrement and it can be called potpourri but it is still excrement. The indelible brand was placed on captured Africans and used every day to break their pride and make them submit to being a slave. Blacks speak out against Whites who feel they are superior but continue destructive practices like using the slur that keeps them inferior and then uses it on another Black person to give them an inferior complex. This effort to stop the use of the slur will be ignored just as many Blacks still consume sugary drinks but will not discover the severity of the damage to their body until years later.

Posted 11/28/2016

SUMMATION.   The word has been used to keep Black and White people divided and now it has caused a division among Black people. Some White people are uninhibited about using the word publicly in the context of its original meaning since Donald Trump has become President of the United States. Younger Whites who have Black friends who use the word and are fans of rap music feel they have the right to say the word as some Black people use it because they hear it in the lyrics of their favorite rap artists who they support and buy their music. This has angered many Blacks and Black rap artists who instruct White people they are not allowed to say the word.

However, this word has been woven into the fabric of America and spread all over the world by White people and more importantly, Black people that know other ethnic groups identify and reference Black people by the word. Many people want to remove the word from language and have it go away but it is too late. It is so deeply entrenched in society that any suggestion to prohibit the word is met with the same opposition NFL players received for not standing for the Flag during the playing of the National Anthem. Blacks who use the word state to other Blacks they have taken ownership of the word but they fail to recognize it still leaves a stain and a stench on Black people. Reducing the power and use of the word will take generations of younger Blacks to object to hearing the word and to challenge other Blacks to not use the word. Silence is golden. Restraint builds character. The seeds for a new beginning for Black people.

The Lease
(New Forms of Marriage)

A decision by President Obama to legalize same-sex marriage opens the door for new forms of marriage with many different options for people. The traditional form of marriage is not under siege from the government and people in same-sex relationships. It is that this standard is no longer the overwhelming choice for many people of today and possibly future generations. In the world of today, people want to make their own decisions they feel are best for their lives and not be restricted to ideas, rules, and laws of people from the past. As time moves on, there are less and less objections to the new forms of marriage that are being accepted by society although, it may be against the law or there is no law for it.

Marriages were once arranged by parents and still are in some countries around the world. In the past, there were marriages made out of necessity. A union was formed by a man and woman to help each other make it through life. There are marriages of convenience where one of the partners are more substantial than the other and it helps the lesser of the two improve their life. The most celebrated form of marriage is from attraction and love where the individuals form an union by decisions derived from emotions to be together the rest of their lives. However, these forms of matrimony are based on one woman and one man but there are forms of marriage where the components are changed.

In some societies, men marry multiple wives and this is becoming a popular form of marriage which is common in Mormon society. It is conceivable that in the future the participants in this type of union can increase to form an economically strong based marriage to build upon to achieve financial independence. The participants will include multiple men and women having multiple children with ability to amass property and start businesses that sustains the group without being dependent on one provider. This is only a few of the non-conventional unions that are existing in the world today. These types of unions take committed people with a broad outlook to achieve their ultimate goals.

A detriment to traditional marriages is divorce. Many people pay more for a divorce than they spent to get married. Settling property, accounts, alimony and child support are the principal subjects of divorce but it is the extraordinary amount of attorney fees, court cost, and taxes that are not expected by couples who want to bring an end to their marriage. It can be a minimal expense for some couples however, for those whose divorce continues to linger on for some time the price of it can become astronomical. Some couples have prenuptial agreements but they are often challenged adding to the court costs. There is a way to avoid the conflict and aggravation.

The use of a lease can be a viable method for individuals to form a union by coming to an agreement on the expectations and length of the arrangement. Living location, children or no children, the responsibility of finances and the purpose for money accrued by the individuals during the lease are significant components of a relationship. It is up to applicable parties to determine what they want the lease to consist of which can include penalties for violating any part of the lease. There can be a provision added to make amendments to the lease before the time of the lease is completed.

Once the lease is expired the participants have the option to walk away or sign a new lease for the same amount of time or a new length of time. They can separate without any court costs, attorney fees, or unexpected expenses because they have agreed on their individual responsibilities and to honor their part in business matters, accounts with balances, and children, if applicable, that is stipulated in the lease. If their time during the lease went well, they have an option to get married but if they want to end their relationship they can leave each other without being divorced. This might be a preparatory endeavor for those who are indecisive about marriage to determine if they are ready for matrimony.

There will likely be a resistance from the courts, attorneys, and the law from this new form of blissful bond because it will significantly affect revenue for the courts, fees for attorneys, and taxes for the law that are received from people going through a divorce. The lease may be attacked with a new law or laws however, this could cause a domino effect that can impact other contracts of different matters. Lawmakers and politicians will have to make a concession on this subject that people change laws because laws do not change people.

Posted 11/29/2016

SUMMATION. The idea of the lease originated from more people choosing to live together rather than binding ties in marriage. Unlike marriage however, there is no alimony or spousal support. Once the relationship ends, all of the unpaid expenses occurred during that time are left to the person who has their name on the accounts. In some cases, it is difficult to find the other person after breaking up, get them into court, and have them pay their share of the expenses. Now, the one person has the sole responsibility of paying off the debts while trying to start a new life. A lease will prevent these situations because both parties will be responsible for all the expenses occurred during the relationship. If it ends, it will be up to the creditors to get payment from the person who is delinquent rather than the other person who was in the the relationship.

These types of situations will continue to happen because young people are waiting longer to get married and are moving in and out of relationships. There are some who have a good job but do not want the burdens that come along with being married while some college graduates are dealing with college debt and trying to keep their head above water. A lease could become needful for anyone entering a relationship or getting married as it can be a carefully thought out plan for all situations that happen during and after the relationship or marriage. It will face opposition from religious sects who will have a moral objection to this type of union because it goes against their beliefs causing couples to be reluctant to enter into it. The apprehension many people have talking about a will is the same way they are going to act toward a lease. They do not want to go through the process but in the end they are glad they have it.

They Fit The Description
(FTD Means Deliver A Black Man To Injustice)

As times have changed from the use of a horse and buggy for transportation to fast vehicles and airplane travel; from the pony express delivering mail to lightening fast information being sent over the Internet on social media sites, some practices remain despite modern advancements. The ability to move about for Black people has always been difficult and challenging even after restrictions were removed. During segregation, *Black Codes* were discriminatory laws used against Black people, particularly Black men and Black boys, so they could be put on the *chain gang* and made to do free labor or hired out into the *contract labor* system where money was exchanged between a contractor and law enforcement while the Black worker received nothing for their work. It remains an odyssey for the Black man of today who draws suspicion on his appearance without knowledge of his character and not being regarded and respected as a human.

Black activists fought to be able to shop in White-owned stores and eat at White-owned restaurants. These were common acts that Blacks saw Whites be able to perform without any problems or resistance. However, once Blacks were allowed to shop and eat at most stores and restaurants by law, the sentiment did not change in most of these businesses. High-end stores do not believe Blacks can afford their merchandise and often humiliate them by having security follow them around the store as they shop or detain them to verify they are valid shoppers or worse, have them arrested for believing they have used a stolen credit card which turns out to be a false allegation.

For a Black man, walking around in America is like walking through a field of land mines. It does not matter who he is, his profession, or stature in society because due to his complexion and characteristics, he fits the description. Charles Belk is a freelance television producer who was accosted by police while walking in Beverly Hills. The police detained Belk for six hours before informing him that he was mistaken for a robbery suspect. Belk, who was walking from a restaurant to his car to check the parking meter, asked but never received a description of the suspect.

Mistaken identity is often used as an excuse for apprehending Black men who are said to fit the description. Oftentimes, it is about arresting a Black man rather than capturing the correct suspect. Tennis pro James Blake was outside his hotel about to proceed to the U.S. Open to complete corporate obligations when he was thrown to the ground and handcuffed by New York City police officers. Blake suffered cuts and bruises from being manhandled by the police. After detaining Blake for 15 minutes, one of the officers made it known that Blake was not their suspect in an identity theft ring. The officers did not apologize to Blake for their wrongful detainment.

The police have cried wolf too often for the continued apprehension of innocent Black men to be a mistake. Violating the rights of Black men is more of a standard practice than accidental behavior by the police. Fit the description has easily been applied in arresting Black men and ignoring their true identity. This vague manner in searching for suspects has caused many Black men to be imprisoned and serve long sentences. Their only connection to the description is that they were Black. Although police officers, district attorneys, and judges carryout these injustices, it is the people who feel secure by these actions that are the reason these violations of human rights continue to exist.

Posted 02/03/2017

SUMMATION. There have been numerous incidents involving Black people having interactions with police that have resulted in fatal conclusions. These are perpetual occurrences that are at the height of topics in society and on social media because most of these incidents have been captured on video. However, there is a long history of police brutality, unlawful detainment, and murders of Black people as well as turning a blind eye to White citizens performing the same heinous acts on Black people. There is no video to those crimes and most reports were distorted in White-owned newspapers. Although Black writers and Black journalists were reporting a more accurate account of these incidents, their articles did not reach the White community or other ethnic groups the way social media has made it possible to be disseminated today.

A new form of a harassment by White people toward Black people is calling the police for matters that are very similar to the *Black Codes*. Police have responded to 911 calls for a Black student sleeping in a study room at a college university; a Black student said to be trespassing on a college campus despite having college identification; a group of Black people barbecuing in a public park; a Black child selling bottled water on a sidewalk. Many Black people believe these calls are being made by Whites in the hopes that police will make an arrest or even worse, a fatal shooting. There are many people who refuse to admit to themselves that the bigotry and discrimination of the past is alive and well today and there are still people who do not want to associate with Black people.

Taking Care Of Self Does
Not Mean You Are Selfish
(Stand Up For "YOUR" Rights)

It is an esteemed virtue for a person to possess the willingness to help others who are in need. This spirit is what connects humans to each other and is often exhibited in an impulsive reactionary manner after seeing a person suffering from a sudden loss or struggling to maintain a basic standard of life. Although there are many who are eager to help others, there are many who have to be prodded to give assistance and support to people who are in an unfortunate situation. They think only of themselves and only the principles in their lives which many people find selfish but it may be a benefit to them that helpful people cannot internalize.

For some, this impassioned need to help other people is to their own detriment. They wake up in the morning with the needs of someone else on their mind and forgetting about their own. Their day may include collecting donations or making donations for the benefit others while their own financial situation is in an overextended state. A restful night of sleep is unattainable from thinking about what to do for others while worrying about what they cannot do for themselves. An unnecessary strain for people already caught up in a struggle while trying to help people who are in an unfortunate predicament but have no plan for getting themselves out of the stressful situation.

This is a strange acceptance for many Black people who feel the need to speak out and protest about issues for other people while they have to attend to their issues themselves because they are ignored by their elected representatives. It is a bad habit that could be attributed to Black slaves who attached themselves with their master and his family because they were treated as part of the family but it was actually what they could do for the family that made them a prize possession. If the master suffered a loss, the Black slave felt sorrow. When the master became ill, the Black slave shared the sickness. However, the master had no objections to selling a family member of the Black slave or retiring an old Black slave to a shack in the woods when they were no longer productive without providing them food and clothing.

Black people have inserted themselves into marches and protests led by other groups while they neglect to lead a march and protest supported by other people for the terrorist act of giving water contaminated with lead to residents of Flint, MI. A show of concern and support for people trying to protect themselves and their land from hazardous environmental decisions by Black people is commendable but they have not shown the same type of concern and support along with being backed by non-Blacks for the positioning of Planned Parenthood facilities in Black communities. This willingness to participate is being an American by standing with other Americans however, they are still being looked upon and treated as less than American.

Taking up one's own issues is not being inconsiderate of others and it is an act of self-preservation. For one to help someone else they must be well themselves and able to provide support of their own. Black people in America are not in a condition to continue to fight for causes that do not bring them any benefit. This has been done in the past as Black men served in the United States Armed Forces and returned home to be disrespected and not able to use the benefits they had earned. Black women marched and protested with the Women's Liberation Movement but it would be the Black woman who would not be able to live with her husband in public housing. Showing concern for others is a spiritual virtue of Black people that is difficult to set aside but taking care of themselves does not make them selfish and it is needed if they are to overcome the atrocities of the past and bring their people to a state of self-reliance, independence, and empowerment.

Posted   02/13/2017

SUMMATION. The spirit of Black people is welcoming and full of acceptance of others and it is in their nature to offer help. This human kindness towards others is a remarkable characteristic that gives them the ability to show forgiveness. However, this natural spirit was corrupted by colonization and slavery which pitted Blacks against each other and intentionally divided Black families for centuries. Out of this developed a kinship, an affection, an endearment to those who oppressed and enslaved Blacks by some of the future generations of Black slaves who were born into these conditions and never knew freedom. Animosity would build between Blacks depending on their relationship to their oppressors. There were some Blacks who were close to their oppressors on a daily basis and they were given the belief that they were family by their captors. In total noncompliance, Blacks who rarely interacted with their oppressors never formed an allegiance or attachment with those who kept them in bondage.

This is why it is easy for some Black people to support other people and their causes while they neglect and ignore their own issues the same way groups do not give any attention to matters important to Black people. Some Blacks are easy to forgive those who commit crimes against them because of centuries of being taught to turn the other cheek through religion by their oppressors and never being able to form a formidable group with power to overcome their condition and stop this submissive behavior. A disruptive mentality was displayed by some Black women who continued to patronize Asian beauty supply stores and nail salons while a group of Black protesters led by Black men demonstrated outside for the disrespect and abuse dealt out to Black women by owners and employees of the businesses. This same attitude will be shown by a segment of Black people who will speak out in opposition of Nike for having Colin Kaepernick be the face of a marketing campaign. Blacks have to develop a mentality to pridefully stand up for themselves as quickly as they support the cause of other groups. They must demand respect and insist on their issues being addressed for them to progress out of this state of disparity and be treated fairly in society.

Faith and Loyalty Does Not Win Championships
(A Change At Quarterback)

An NFL team that has a good quarterback is reluctant to move on from this player in spite of not winning a Super Bowl with the quarterback for several seasons. The fans have formed an allegiance with the player and believe this is the quarterback that will help them win a championship. This faith and loyalty is a great show of support to the player but sometimes a team can stay with a quarterback too long and the players may need a new voice and a different style of play. The Tampa Bay Buccaneers recognized this and made a change at coach by replacing Tony Dungy with Jon Gruden who won a Super Bowl with the players Dungy had coached. Dungy would move on to the Indianapolis Colts to win a championship with Peyton Manning at quarterback.

It comes a time when a team has to move on and look to the future irregardless of the skepticism it will face. The Baltimore Colts traded Hall of Famer Johnny Unitas to the San Diego Chargers to get younger at quarterback as the veteran was nearing the end of his career. Joe Montana was traded by the San Francisco 49ers because his backup was the quarterback of the future. Steve Young replaced Montana at quarterback and led the 49ers to a win in Super Bowl XXIX. Montana would end his career with the Kansas City Chiefs leading them to the playoffs twice before he retired. Andrew Luck was drafted by the Colts who would trade Manning to the Denver Broncos to make room for their quarterback of the future. Manning would win one of the two Super Bowls he played in with the Broncos before he retired.

Trading a quarterback can be good for the player and the team as it can motivate players to play better after seeing a long tenured player at the most prestigious position in football get traded. It can benefit the player as well as it did Craig Morton who was traded by Dallas to the Broncos after playing in back-to-back Super Bowls in 1970 and 1971 for the Cowboys. Morton would later play in another Super Bowl with the Broncos against the Cowboys and the quarterback who took his place, Roger Staubach. Jim Plunkett would join the Oakland Raiders after being released by the 49ers. Plunkett would play in two championships with the Raiders and be a Super Bowl MVP.

For many teams, the quarterback position is a question unanswered for next season while for a few teams it is solidified. Although, it might not should be as in the case of the Chargers who are moving to Los Angeles and bringing along Philip Rivers to continue to be their quarterback after 12 exceptional seasons but he has failed to lead the team to a Super Bowl. Andy Dalton will start at quarterback for the Cincinnati Bengals after failing in 4 attempts to win a playoff game. Matt Ryan was quarterback for the Atlanta Falcons during their historical collapse in Super Bowl LI. Although he has won 3 playoff games, Ryan has lost 5 playoff games and has never established a level of consistency and a winning atmosphere for the team during his tenure. These are all good quarterbacks whose services may be better used by another team.

As long as teams shower their quarterbacks with loads of money, they will not only be invested with large contracts but reluctant to trade their quarterback if they are unable to win. San Diego signed Ryan Leaf to a major contract without receiving any benefits for their commitment from the temperamental player; the

Raiders signed JaMarcus Russell to a monumental deal but were reward with no success from the lackluster quarterback; the Jacksonville Jaguars are still waiting for results from Blake Bortles after 3 seasons. Support from the team and loyalty from the fans for their quarterback allows camaraderie to exist but refusing to change allows for futility and losing to persist.

Posted   02/15/2017

SUMMATION.   There are several NFL teams starting the season with the same quarterback who played the final game for them last year or was a member of the team. This includes the New England Patriots who lost in the Super Bowl to the Philadelphia Eagles. Coach Bill Belichick appeared to have his quarterback of the future but was forced to trade Jimmy Garoppolo to the San Francisco 49ers and stand pat with Tom Brady as his starting quarterback. An aging Brady is still playing at a high level winning MVP of the season last year however, Belichick may have seen the future in Garoppolo who had the ability to help the Patriots continue to play at a championship level.

Some teams are starting the season with a different quarterback in hopes of winning a Super Bowl. The Minnesota Vikings gave an enormous contract to Kurt Cousins to be their quarterback and help them go further in the playoffs this year. There are some teams who are using veterans quarterbacks to groom rookies such as the Cleveland Browns starting Tyrod Taylor ahead of rookie Baker Mayfield, their quarterback of the future. Meanwhile, the New York Jets traded Teddy Bridgewater to the New Orleans Saints in a decision to start Sam Darnold at quarterback. Change can help some teams become winners while other teams choose to stay with familiarity. Such as the Jacksonville Jaguars who finally made it to the playoffs last year with Blake Bortles as their quarterback and have him starting this year. There is anticipation for Andrew Luck to return from injury and finally lead the Colts to a championship. In an attempt to return to glory, the Los Angeles Raiders made a significant change at coach giving Jon Gruden a lucrative contract in hopes his experience can and bring them a Super Bowl championship as he did the Tampa Bay Buccaneers.

An Act Too Hard To Follow
(Artists Unworthy of Support)

It is a memorable experience to see the evolution of a musical artist. From being unknown to becoming world renowned. A famous artist that diehard fans were able to watch develop from an opening act that most people did not come to see but were stunningly entertained by the performance of the artist. There was a desire to be great in the artist that connected with some in the audience who became supporters of the artist despite their early singles not being regarded as hits and the release of albums that did not break the top 50 or top 100 on the album charts. Once the artist had a major hit, their core fans enjoyed the success along with the artist.

As the artists matures into their career, some of them do not highly regard their diehard fans with the same affection they received in the beginning from their supporters. These artists who were struggling for attention when they started now feel they are above their fans and are arrogantly disposed to believe the fans are fortunate to see them perform. They have this attitude because they have attained *"hot right now"* fans who will be gone when the next *"hot right now"* artist emerges and their next single and album is not a hit. Fame and fortune has caused them to overlook fans who sat in the front seats to see them perform when they were not making money and now pay astronomical prices for tickets just to get into the arenas for their concerts.

After standing in line, the supportive fans take their expensive seats. They are made to wait an half hour to hours for their artist to take the stage. The same artist who was eager to take the stage at the start of their career and sometimes begged to be allowed to perform on stage. Fans are somewhat to blame for this aspect because they pay extravagant prices for tickets to a concert and complain about the artist being late to show up on stage after watching them perform but they continue to support the artist by buying music and more tickets to concerts after the artist has not shown any remorse and correction of their behavior.

Once the artist takes the stage, their act will be abbreviated because of their lateness. Instead of trying to give their core fans their money's worth in a short amount of time, they will give a lackluster performance of their songs and ask for crowd participation by holding the microphone toward the audience. This is an insult to the fans who have paid and waited to see the artist perform. Fans are responsible for the continuance of this type of performance because they would not accept going to a restaurant and be asked by the chef to help cook their meal. Some people paid astronomical prices for their tickets and want to see the artist perform not listen to people around them singing off key.

For true fans supporting their favorite performers is an act too hard to follow. Though the fan has stayed informed about the artist for years, there are now alternative methods for the fan to enjoy grand performances by the artist who showed their heart was truly in their art. There are Internet sites that have videos and recordings of the artist that remind the fan why they started supporting the artist. The greatest hits of the artist can be purchased to be enjoyed alone or in the company of other diehard fans of the artist. A great number of artist do act professionally and perform in a manner that their fans get more than their money's worth. These are the artists the fans should continue to support.

Posted 02/17/2017

SUMMATION.   A number of music artists are learning the adage *"the customer is always right"* as they are having to cancel tour dates due to lack of ticket sales. These artists are debuting albums and are expecting to perform in sold out arenas but fans are refusing to pay astronomical prices for tickets to see a sub par show. There are artists who show up for the money but do not want to earn the money. Fans are waiting to spend their money on the concerts featuring artists who give great performances and who love entertaining an audience which make them leave the concert knowing they got their money's worth.

Musical artists who know how to entertain an audience can tour for years without putting out a single or an album. They perform their old hits with the intention of exciting the crowd and more importantly, appearing on stage at an appropriate time so as not to make the audience frustrated from waiting unnecessarily. These are artists who actually sing at their concerts along with the artists who dance and the artists who play musical instruments. The fans do not want to see artists go through a routine without giving any effort while using recorded music the entire show. Artists have to understand that concerts are events that fans have worked hard to buy the ticket and may have taken off work to attend the show. They have made an effort to make the concert and they want the artists to give an effort on the stage. If not, ticket sales will continue to be lackluster and concert dates will continue to be canceled.

The Sacrifice For The New Frontier
(Antarctica)

Ice is melting on the southern polar caps and large chunks of it are breaking off and floating away causing sea levels to rise. Only scientific researchers and conscientious observers know the significance of this metamorphosis. A land that has only been home to very few human inhabitants and consisting of government research stations is now being exposed. Many believe the cause is global warming but it may not be from negligence of corporations. The change occurring in Antarctica could be the intentions of those in power in an attempt to lay claim on the continent that is rich in natural resources and build it up to be the super power of the future that rules the world.

President Donald Trump and President Vladimir Putin have considerable interest in the vast continent because of the large oil reserves beneath the layers of solid ice. It can be perceived that these two unfavorable leaders want to be the first to drill for oil on Antarctica to substantially increase their personal wealth. However, these two men, who do not want to answer to anyone and make up their own rules as they go along, may have formed an alliance to set up a new civilization and establish a government in a new world for their people. Although, they are supposed to be adversaries and this is only speculation, it is not inconceivable that plans are being made for Antarctica to be the future home for Whites and all people of European descent.

At the beginning of the millennium, there was a concerted effort by America and European governments to get into Africa. A vast continent with a plentiful extent of natural resources enticed the foreign governments to enter Africa by forcing wars throughout the continent to gain control of the abundant environment, specifically oil. Studies were done on melanin in the skin of people of color and soon products flooded retail markets that were made to protect the skin from the sun. These products were made for one group of people as people of color have the natural protection of melanin for their skin. Whites suffer burns from too much sun and are susceptible to forms of skin cancer. The hot climate of Africa was too much for the products as Whites learned how harsh of a life they would endure on the continent. Despite its wealth of natural resources it became less desirable to Whites while the Chinese and the Japanese, people with melanin in their skin, have forged their way into many African countries.

The White population is decreasing and unable to maintain a birth rate comparable to people of color which makes the perception of the Antarctica plan possible. Islands in the Caribbean have seen an influx of Chinese and Japanese governments and businesses seemingly, without any contention from the American government and any major news coverage by the American media to lands in close proximity to the borders of the United States. As Sea levels rise from the melting ice of Antarctica, it is being proclaimed that coastal states will have land submerged, maybe the complete state of Florida. There is a belief by many that the flooding of New Orleans was a test run for submerging a city and then disperse its citizens to other cities in the United States without providing them with sufficient assistance to return home.

It is possible that the geographical map will be changed as sea levels continue to rise. New York,

Washington, D.C., and the Carolina's could be consumed by the ocean and Atlanta, with a major airport, could become the major city on the east coast. Chicago could become the future New York City and St. Louis may be the new capitol of the United States. This is possibly the reason crime, poverty, lack of schools, unemployment, and incarceration are allowed to persist in these cities so Blacks can easily be displaced and overtaken during this future Reconstruction. Most of the west coast will also be covered which would leave Texas as the largest state of the remaining states in the Union.

Islands in the Caribbean may be completely covered by the Atlantic Ocean which may lead to many of their population coming to the United States and making people of color the majority in the country. Although the complexion of the masses may be changed, Whites will still be in power because they own most of the corporations, utilities, and transportation companies and some owners will make the sacrifice for the new frontier by leaving the United States and moving their businesses to Antarctica. This is similar to White businesses leaving Black cities and communities causing economic hardship for those in the area. Initially, people will be dispersed around the world and those left in the United States may struggle to survive. A new form of colonization may come into existence as people may voluntary go to Antarctica to survive at the expense of their human rights, freedom, and their family.

It has been shown throughout history how people of color are adaptable to different climates but the climate of Antarctica is ideal for Whites and Europeans. They are descendants of a people who lived in the Caucasus Mountains for thousands of years before migrating into Northern Africa. The Caucasus

Mountains are located between the Black Sea to the west and the Caspian Sea to the east and are occupied by Russia, Georgia, Azerbaijan, and Armenia. President Trump and President Putin may have a plan to return their people to an accommodating habitat and environment that is void of the problems that America and Europe are facing in some of its cities today. Antarctica is a model place for their people because most of the land is white, most of the bears are white, and most of the people in the future will be White.

Posted 02/17/2017

SUMMATION.   There is speculation that global warming is having an effect on Antarctica. The continent is showing the most greenery that has been seen on the land in the last 50 years. A noticeable loss in the penguin population is attributed to the increase in water temperature which is said to be the cause of melting ice, breaking icebergs, and shrinking glaciers. This adds freshwater into the oceans causing sea levels to rise. Many people believe this is having an effect on the weather as storms have become more violent. Hurricanes, typhoons, and tornadoes leave massive destruction in their wake but severe thunderstorms are able to produce flash flooding because of the increased sea level.

Meanwhile, Russia is increasing its presence on the continent. It is expanding the development of bases put in place under the Soviet Union to add a global positioning system. America already has a GPS on the continent. China is also taking an interest in expansion on Antarctica by building a fourth research base and looking for a location to construct a fifth. Scientists predicted 50 years ago the potential for rising sea levels as the result of melting ice caps. This history is known by leaders of countries who are looking to lay claim on the natural resources of the continent. It is time people pay attention to what is going on with Antarctica.

Why Not Me?
(The C-word)

It can be like hearing a death sentence from a judge to many people when their doctor informs them they have cancer. Their world is thrown off balance and shaken into disarray that it may take years for them to stabilize it. They have seen this debilitating disease take the lives of family members, friends, and popular people after going through strenuous radiation and chemotherapy treatments. A sense of inevitability is fallen into by the patient who forms a belief they will follow the same pattern of others they have witnessed succumb to the disease. Then they ask the self-deprecating question, *"Why me?"*

The question is never asked or thought about when one wins the lottery, land a very lucrative job, or get a scholarship to a prestigious university. It is only given credence when something detrimental happens in one's life that is a setback and they do not have an explanation for this occurrence. This attitude is taken without understanding that if one is able to avoid harm, injury, and sickness that it will befall another person. No one asks the question, *"Why them?"* when they see a person struck by tragedy. Their instant response is to give sympathy and support to the person who is enduring hardship.

A person who learns they have cancer will feel trepidation about their future and it will take some time to acknowledge they have the disease. The sooner the person can accept the diagnosis the more appropriately and advantageously they can attack the disease at an early stage before it can do severe damage to the person and spread throughout the body. A positive attitude and encouraging support from family and friends is a medicine that is as equally important as radiation, chemotherapy, and immunotherapy treatments. A fabulous source of strength can be found in surviving cancer patients and people having their own battle with cancer who can bring an energy, support, and determination to beat the disease.

Momentarily feeling distressed for one's self is understandable but the question that enters the mind should not be *"Why me?"* but *"Why not me?"* It may be this person can be an inspiration to others by the way they are fighting disease and they always have a positive outlook despite severe reactions from their treatments. The person can bring light to their family the necessity for prevention and help them be less susceptible in case the disease is hereditary. No one chooses to get a cold. Most people take shots to prevent having the flu. There is no one who wants to hear the c-word but just as people look to recover from a cold and the flu, they should have the outlook they will recover from cancer and not falter at the mention of its name and ask *"Why me?"*

Posted 02/28/2017

SUMMATION. The c-word is not the death sentence it has been in the past. People are surviving the disease and the treatments and able to go on with their lives. However, there are still some people succumbing to the disease becoming terminally ill or having the disease return after successful treatments. After the battle with cancer, it takes a person time to resume with their life. Their body has to heal and reform to its new condition from surgeries and several treatments that may have changed the texture of their hair, caused them to have restrictive movement, or having to replace their teeth and adjusting to a new diet.

Those who were restricted to their home by disease will have to slowly return the world. It will be mentally challenging and for some, physically demanding. Trying to go back to work, become sociable, and learning to drive or getting around on their own are routine things easily accomplished in the past but may have to be done tentatively, one step at a time. Although a person may look healthy and appear to be doing well, their lives have been interrupted by a serious illness and they may try to get up to speed with their life right away by catching up with family and friends, catching up with the latest styles in fashion and travel, and catching up with the many medical bills tallied up from medicine, treatment, and procedures. A temperate, steady walk back into life can prevent a person from becoming overwhelmed and mentally despondent.

The Great Mistake
(The Failure of Integration)

Those who fought for equal rights during the Civil Rights Era feel they achieved great accomplishments and took significant strides in improving the lives of Blacks in America. They made extraordinary sacrifices that resulted in many of them being beaten, thrown in jail, or losing their life from being on the frontline for fighting against an opposition who did not recognize them as American citizens or as being human. A struggle for natural rights ensued in a country that used the ancestors of the Black activists to become a powerful nation and were reluctant to allow their descendants to become a powerful people who could determine paths for their own people and future generations.

The objective to achieve equal rights was not to share resources equally with other groups but to be provided with resources that equaled what other groups received to educate, train, and uplift their people. For their dire efforts and faithful contributions, they received the system of integration. After dutifully striving and leading the way for change in America, they would have to share in a system with those who opposed them and would benefit the least. Civil rights laws afforded more resources to White women and the disabled than the Blacks who had protested and had legal precedent established in courts.

Although many Blacks saw this as an opportunity for Black students to get a better education by attending better schools with people who hated and despised them, it was at the expense of Black teachers, school administrators and superintendents who would lose their jobs. Few would be offered positions at integrated schools but it would be in much lesser roles than they had at segregated schools. An incorrect assessment about this period is that all Blacks were for integration but Black teachers, school administrators and superintendents were not because they knew they would lose their jobs. However, civil rights leaders believed the sacrifice of a few was to the greater good of the entire race.

This sacrifice of Black teachers, school administrators and superintendents would result in race destructive consequences that still exist today. The Black educators knew that Black children should be taught by Black teachers. Most schools refused to let White children learn from Black teachers and be under the supervision of Black administrators and superintendents. This became a detriment to Black children who were only educated by White teachers and overseen by White administrators and superintendents, therefore, they equated them with being smart and intelligent. Black people who worked as janitors and in food service may have been former educators but they were not held with high esteem by the Black students. A Black child that was smart and intelligent was seen as acting White to other Black children because they resembled who was teaching them and rarely saw educated Black adults in authoritative roles.

Integration led many Blacks to believe everything Whites owned was substantially better than what Blacks owned though, Blacks had built respectable communities during segregation. However, some Blacks felt the need to spend their money in stores and restaurants owned by Whites and abandoned Black businesses they had frequented during segregation. This phenomena is known as *"the*

White man's ice is colder" and marked the beginning of the end for Black communities. The only institution left in Black communities is the Black church because it is no threat to the White economy as most Black churches do their banking with White financial institutions.

There are some Blacks today who see integration as a failure and is at the core for the demise of Black communities and the deprave condition of Black people. They do not revere Black civil rights activists who wanted integration as their parents and grandparents. This can be recognized by many Blacks not voting despite Black civil rights activists working tirelessly for the Voting Rights Act. They choose the option to abstain from voting rather than to participate in a system that is structured to get them in a penal institution rather than an academic or business institution or to vote for a candidate that has their own agenda for Black people or no agenda for Black people or has no regard for the agenda of Black people.

History presents integration as a significant turning point in America for Black people but for many of them it was a downward turn that has sent them on a constant descent in a country that only wanted the services of their ancestors but never wanted them to be citizens of the country. Integration was presented as a great opportunity for Black people to become part of America however, they had always been part of the country but never received value for their worth or benefits from their work. As the old Black generation honors integration as a great achievement, the younger Black generation abhors integration as the great mistake.

Posted 03/06/17

SUMMATION.   Black people of the Civil Rights Era made the same mistake as Black people during Reconstruction. In both periods, Black leaders and activists were trying to improve the conditions of Black people by stating they should have equal rights as afforded them by the Constitution. The problem with this is the people who had their rights according to the Constitution were also the same people who made changes to law and enforced the law. Instead of the honorable Black people working tirelessly to become part of an American society where they were not wanted, they should have tried to get land for Black people to live separately from Whites just as America granted the Native-Americans.

Many White people have made it clear since Donald Trump became President that they are not happy interacting with Black people and would rather live with their own people. This is why Blacks should have received their own land because since slavery ended, Whites have tried to remain separate from Blacks. However, Black people fight to live among White people and they suffer as does the Black community. For this reason, Black people as a group have not progressed since slavery ended. They continue to struggle to be part of an American society that does not want them instead of building a Black society that America beckons and courts rather than pushing them away.

"I fear I am integrating my people into a burning house" - Martin Luther King, Jr.

Acceptance and Respect
(A Gay Right)

As people push forward to have the rights and freedom that are accustomed to others, there is a lack of understanding being given to those of privilege by those who were misunderstood. Activism for gay rights has brought about information of the lifestyle for outsiders; a change of perception of gay people; laws that entitle gay people to live as other citizens in America since the turn of the century. The Rainbow Coalition has enabled people with different sexual preferences to no longer be a hidden thread in the fabric of America but now a profound color and emblem in the culture of America.

With this outpouring of acceptance and respectability for the gay lifestyle has come an attitude of protest for anyone opposing the views of gay people. This opposition is accused of delivering hate speech and exhibiting homophobia from gay proponents for expressing their beliefs and points against the lifestyle without disrespecting gay people. There is a notion by gay people that their lifestyle should be accepted by all and questioned by no one. People who eat meat may not like the vegetarian lifestyle and speak in opposition of it but respect those who live it. Vegetarians should not be prohibited for living their lifestyle neither should they demonize those who do not accept their way of life and speak up for their own rights.

The battle for equal rights for people of the gay and LGBT community is often equated with the struggle for civil and human rights of Black people. This is an error in rationalization because the world, governments, and religion consorted in controlling, owning, and benefiting from the attributes and abilities of Black people. Only religion openly restricted homosexuality but allowed it to exist secretly within its structure without facing the vile wrath and persecution that Black people endured. Gay people reached positions in life before acceptance of their lifestyle was prevalent and laws of tolerance were passed. Black people are still limited and harassed despite the passage of equal opportunity laws. The gay lifestyle can be disguised and hidden but the complexion of a Black person is as visible as the sun during the day and the moon at night.

Black people faced strong opposition in their protest for their civil and human rights to keep them *"in their place"* whereas the opposition with gay people is a disagreement with their lifestyle. Forcing people to go against their beliefs will only prevent them from reaching a reasonable position of acceptance and respect. It is through information, time to adjust, and understanding that the disagreement will remain but opposing views will be respected. At some point, there minds will close and fixate on responding to the opposition with the same amount or greater force that has been directed at their people. A gay right should not be imposed on people, it should be respected by all people.

Posted 03/09/2017

SUMMATION. Great strides were made by the LGBTQ community during the presidency of Barack Obama who championed the rights of the group. The President supported the law giving same-sex couples the right to marry and tried to persuade other countries to change their views on people who prefer a sexual relationship with someone of the same gender. Under President Donald Trump, the focus has been shifted away from gay rights however, attitudes toward members of the LGBTQ community are now more acceptable and tolerable. Although the group still faces some opposition, a young generation is being taught an inclusive ideology that is helping the group blend into society.

Old world views are being challenged and overturned. India's highest court said the LGBTQ community has the same fundamental rights as citizens in a milestone verdict that decriminalizes consensual gay sex. As people became tolerable toward members of LGBTQ community into society, the group must also appreciate and respect those who object to their lifestyle. Laws do not change people's attitudes, especially when the beliefs they were taught have been passed down for generations. Deeply ingrained views and practices cannot be changed in a day with a pen. For a society to exist together peacefully, there must be acceptance, respect, and tolerance from all groups of people.

The Silent Assassin
(Sexual Abuse In The Black Community)

Their is a behavior in Black society that has permeated generation after generation without being challenged by Black elders, Black parents, and Black children. As allegations of sexual abuse in the past are being brought forth by the apparent victims, there is a more sinister problem that persists in the Black community. A reluctance to acknowledge or report these deplorable vile acts by Black families has created an environment that allows this deviant behavior to exist and continue without being exposed or confronted. This reprehensible silence is just as much of a violation as the sexual assaults.

The neglect by some Black family members to bring attention to heinous acts against other family members may result from them being victims themselves whose violations were kept secret. It is not uncommon for spouses and children to have mates and parents who were sexually abused as children but it is hard to accept that some of them are the perpetrators of sexual abuse instead of silencers who decide it is better to bury the acts of impropriety not realizing their family member will have to live with the deviant acts that they will not acknowledge.

In many Black families, the fear of any revelation of sexual abuse will bring shame upon the family and blemish the family's name. There is more importance put on the reputation of the family name and the image of the family member than the accountability of the family for the well-being of the family member who has been violated. However, the sexually abused family member lives with shame as their family carries on a pretense of a normal family structure while the life of their violated relative is forever changed and will never be the same.

A plausible reason to how this illicit behavior was integrated into the lives of Black people could be from the results of their ancestors in colonization and slavery. Africans and Black slaves were violated at the will of colonists and proponents of slavery without a mother and a father, a wife and a husband, and any family member being able to provide protection. These abused people developed a mentality to suffer in silence and live with the possibility to escape in the future. Some would want to avenge the demeaning acts but it could come at a consequence of certain death for many or all of them or they would be separated by being sold to different owners in different states.

It is imperative that the silence that enables these demonic acts to permeate and the practice of sexual abuse be removed from the conscious of Black people. This epidemic effects all groups of society and enabled it to continue by silence of family members. A spouse is usually the one who suffocates the plea of a child for help because they do not want to face financial hardship if their mate is the violator. Their rationale is it is better to remain quiet with a roof over their head, food to eat, and clothes on their backs than to reveal their mate is a sexual deviant, get help for their child, and become a one-earning income family.

This sickness is detrimental to the future of Black people. Sexual abuse in the Black community corrupts valuable minds that have the possibility of helping Black people out of a condition of despair and rise to a state of respectability. There are many who have been able to overcome their attacks and become successful but are still conflicted by their abusers and the assaults just as those who were seriously affected from being sexually abused and have been on a downward spiral since they were violated. Now is the time to shine the light on this silent assassin and eradicate it from the lives of Black people, the Black family, and the Black community so their seeds can grow and bear a harvest that can build a Nation with the ability to sustain itself.

Posted 03/13/2017

SUMMATION. Although sex is prevalent in the music, movies, and social media that the Black community views as entertainment, it is still a taboo subject in Black families. In today's social climate, children are introduced or exposed to sex at an early period in their lives. Some Black parents choose not too address the subject because they are not comfortable talking about it with their young child. However, the subject of sex must be approached by Black parents so as to prevent their children from being influenced by receiving the wrong information. The young child is corrupted and may start performing sexual acts before they are mature and have a knowledgeable understanding of sex.

It is also difficult for Black families to discuss sexual abuse when the victim and the perpetrator are relatives. In order to avoid embarrassment and shame being brought on the family name, the situation is not talked about and becomes a family secret. The problem is not addressed which will effect the victim in to adulthood until it is dealt with professionally or talking to someone who has experience about the subject outside of the family. If not addressed proper, the victim will have problems forming relationships in the future. Protecting the perpetrator only gives them the opportunity to continue this indecent behavior. This person has to be removed from the family in spite of how much they will be missed to prevent the family from suffering more pain. They also need professional help and not allowed to have their deplorable discretion hidden by the family. In order to have strong and vibrant Black communities, Black families cannot allow their seeds to be abused and expect them to grow into adults without character flaws and mental issues.

An Unforeseen Struggle
(Fighting Cancer)

After significant thought and finally accepting being diagnosed with a potentially fatal disease that has taken the lives of family, friends, co-workers, and people who have provided entertainment and thrilling moments in sports, a person is in a vulnerable position that they are unable to correct their condition by going to their local pharmacy to fill a prescription or buying an over-the-counter product or receiving an injection from their general family doctor for a remedy. They seek a knowledgeable practitioner of medicine who studies cancer and who can provide a treatment that can possibly cure their illness after they have built up their optimism while also conceding they may be facing the conclusion of their life.

Receiving the proper care to battle cancer for patients depends on selecting a well-informed doctor and relying on their intelligence and expertise on the disease. Doctors are chosen by recommendations from other doctors or family and friends or by the health insurance company of the patient. The last method of selection is not based on the experience of the doctor but the health coverage of the patient which provides them with a list of doctors who are in the patients network that the insurance company will pay a greater percentage of the fees and service for treatment. A more desirable and knowledgeable doctor who is chosen by the patient but not in their health coverage network will be very expensive and unaffordable for the patient. This is when the patient learns that health care is a business and is less concerned about the well-being of a patient.

Medical treatment for patients is implemented by an assembly line process similar to an automotive oil change shop inserting the same grade of oil into every vehicle that comes in for service. There is no consideration taken into account by doctors of the chemical structure of the patient who will receive the same treatment as patients before them because they have the same form of cancer. This is in disregard of whether the patient lived or died or had adverse reactions from the treatment. It appears doctors are reluctant to deviate from the process that authorizes certain methods of treatment to be used for forms of cancer in people who need different medical care and treatment.

A reason for this is that choice of treatment is sometimes not decided by doctors or anyone with medical training. *(Read the forms that patients sign to allow treatment from doctors and medical facilities. Decisions are sometimes made by people with other than medical knowledge).* Doctors will stipulate the form of treatment they will prescribe for the patient but unless the patient asks or objects they will not know their are other options. Many doctors will not offer alternative options for the patient and this may be due to the cost-effective management of the medical facility and the insurance company of the patient. The cure is based on cost, it is not based on whether it will cure the patient.

This is a perplexing time for a person whose world has been turned upside down and they look for guidance from those who have studied and practiced medicine to help stabilize it. However, being too trustworthy could be to their detriment. The patient has to become diligent in finding the right doctors, medical facilities, and form of treatment in spite of their emotional stress. They have to understand their health coverage and learn what their insurance company will pay toward their treatment, medical care, and medical supplies. It may benefit the patient to make changes in their health coverage so benefits will be afforded doctors and medical facilities of their choice.

Choosing a doctor may be a difficult responsibility but a patient has to understand it is their body and they will make the final decisions. It may take the help of family and friends to do research on doctors and different forms of treatment. Some patients are reluctant to have 2nd, 3rd, and 4th opinions but they must realize they are fighting cancer and the medical treatment alone will not work if there is no belief in the cure. Battling with doctors over the proper treatment will be an unforeseen struggle for most patients but it is a necessary battle for their life because they may have only one opportunity to get it right.

Posted 03/28/2017

SUMMATION. For awhile in America, doctors made house calls to examine their patients. This was during a time when most people did self-doctoring because their was not a doctor in the area or the office was too far away or they could not pay the doctor for services. The reason many doctors made house calls was to drum up business and to show people they were competent in providing medical care and to introduce people to modern medicine. Doctors would allow patients who could not pay the full price for medical treatment to make payments. This was a business tactic used by doctors to accommodate their patients, who they knew had families, for the next time they needed care.

The relationship between doctor and patient has been infiltrated by insurance and pharmaceutical companies. Care and concern for the patient has been pushed aside by these companies to assure themselves a profitable bottom line. Patients who have paid their monthly insurance premiums responsibly are oftentimes put in a precarious position when they have to find a doctor in their network who makes them comfortable and who they have confidence in treating their illness. This is at a time when patients are trying to understand and determine the best treatment for their illness while their insurance company is deciding what medical treatment will be approved. Patients have to be proactive with their healthcare, this means being informed about their illness and the coverage provided by their insurance company. Healthcare is now a business concerned with payment and profit whether the patient survives or not.

An Easy Method of Choosing Stocks
(A Simple Introduction To The Stock Market)

Investing in the stock market fills many people with trepidation because it is a foreign language to them that they do not understand and they are fearful of losing their hard-earned money. They are content with opening a savings account at a bank and depositing their money in it for safe-keeping while the bank uses their money to collect profits and they accrue a small amount of interest from their savings account. This does not concern them because they have a retirement plan at their job that will benefit them in the future. However, it consists of stocks but they let someone else choose investments at the initial setup of their retirement plan then rarely monitor it or make changes to it.

Being negligent and too trusting in a another person's ability is a pattern of behavior that will lead many to financial difficulty in the future. Refusing to take financial responsibility of income and savings is the same as letting a house go without maintenance. It may still be intact but it is worth nothing. A strategy is needed so years of hard work will not be for nothing and money invested has been hard at work accumulating interest that has built a retirement portfolio filled with substantial funds. This is the desire for most people but they are fearful of approaching the matter because of their lack of knowledge of financial investments. They will rely their future upon hope rather than sound investments.

Watching business shows and listening to financial analysts confuses most people and fills them with more apprehension. They do not know any brokers, what stocks to invest in, and where to start. In actuality, they are more familiar with several stocks than they realize. An easy method for choosing stocks for the novice is to make a list of where they are spending their money. This will include utilities, the products they buy, the stores they shop at, the restaurants they eat at, and the brands that the potential investor has formed a relationship with being a customer for years with the company.

The choice of a utility stock is a simple introduction to the stock market because these are usually monthly expenses for services used such as water, power, and phone. These are companies that have been around for years and will continue to be in business in the future because they provide services that people need and use on a daily basis. Risks are low for these stocks and large gains are minimal but they are good investments over time. Investing in a utility stock means the investor becomes a shareholder of a company they are paying every month as well as their neighbors and friends. So they are not only contributing to the profits of the company, they are also contributing to their investment. Being a customer can also help the investor notice if the company is experiencing a downturn that can help them make a decision on whether to keep the stock or sell it.

Investing in some of these stocks are as easy as going online to pay a monthly bill. On the homepage of the company stock of choice there is an *"Investor Relations"* tab on the site that will give instructions on how to invest in the company. For other companies, there are online discount brokerage firms where shares in the company can be purchased at a minimal fee. There is no need for a broker (who will charge commissions that will reduce investment gains) unless the potential investor is still unsure about investing in stocks. Utility stocks are a good place to start but the same principle to choose other stocks can be used by the investor by being a customer of a company however, they may face more risk and greater volatility.

Another method to use for investing in stocks is dividend investment programs (DRIPS) that allow investing in stocks without buying a full share of stock. Many companies have these programs and some allow investments as low as $10. Investing in stocks does not have to be complicated as companies are in business to make money and so are investors who invest in stocks. If a potential investor pays attention to their spending and purchasing patterns as well as the spending habits of other people, it can help them become a savvy investor and with further study and practice they can become a successful investor. Failing at the stock market is not from loss of money, it is from failing to take the opportunity to make money in the stock market.

Posted 03/31/2017

SUMMATION. Many people are apprehensive and reluctant of buying stocks because they do not have an understanding of how the stock market works. They would rather take that money and play the lottery or go to a casino or horse track to gamble or fantasy sports. The money lost in these ventures could be making money for them in the stock market. It is not a guarantee that money will not be lost on stocks but a sound strategy monitored properly can produce positive results. People are not aware of the investment opportunities that present themselves because they are either too busy spending money or too concerned about saving money.

Nike stock dipped at the announcement of Colin

Kaepernick being the face of their *"Just Do It"* advertising campaign. The stock price of some other sports apparel companies also dropped at the same time. People in support of Kaepernick were planning to go out and buy Nike items while those who were in opposition were refusing to buy Nike products in the future. An investment opportunity presented itself with the low stock prices that most of these people probably missed. Instead of Kaepernick supporters buying Nike apparel, they should have bought Nike stock and those who are are infuriated with Nike should have bought the stock of its competitors. In only a few days, Nike stock had increased higher than when its priced took a dip.

The Sickness Of It All
(Chemotherapy and Radiation)

The effects of chemotherapy and radiation are devastating and debilitating for the patient who will have a life-altering experience. There is no way to avoid sickness, although it can be limited or made less painful; there is no way to avoid hair loss although, it may grow back and sometimes better than what it replaced; there is no way to avoid weakness until strength returns in about a day or two before the next treatment and the daunting process starts all over again. A change of appearance will occur from blotches and irritations affecting the skin that will need special soaps, creams, and lotions to protect its sensitive texture. Weight loss can be distressing as clothes will no longer fit properly and there is a constant struggle to adjust to a body that is constantly reducing in size.

A patient has to have a strong will to endure chemotherapy and radiation, sometimes given on the same day, then be prepared for the sickness that will come a day or two later that will consist of cramping and vomiting with the inability to keep food and drink down. Weakness will set in but it will be difficult to find a comfortable position to get some rest. There will be times that are tolerable and there will be times that are unbearable. The patient never knows how severe the sickness will be until it occurs no matter the preparation taken by the patient which may include receiving relief medication from their doctor and following the same routine of a previous treatment where only light sickness ensued. Feeling relieve from the sickness releasing its hold on the body is like the sun becoming visible in the sky after days of dark clouds have delivered violent lightening and thunder storms.

There will be adverse conditions arise that could possibly include sores in the mouth and difficulty swallowing and veins stressed from treatment and dehydration. At this time, aids and medical devices will be attached to the body for the convenience of the patient and medical personnel so daily functions and medical procedures can still be accomplished and administered to the patient without causing intolerable discomfort. A feeding tube may be necessary for a patient to help keep up strength if they cannot swallow or experience pain while eating from sores in the mouth. This is convenient for the patient that may also need a port for veins that have been overworked from IV use. A port allows blood to be withdrawn and chemotherapy applied without affecting denigrated veins. Although these are helpful and needed, the patient has a feeling of being other than human and looking at themselves as being mutant-like that lowers their spirits and makes them become reclusive.

Despite the usefulness of the aids and medical devices along with the chemotherapy and radiation working on the cancer, a walk past a mirror can be a shock to the patient who cannot recognize their own reflection. The patient looks deep into the mirror trying to find themselves but chemotherapy, radiation, and surgeries has drastically changed the image they have known all of their life. A realization sets in that they will never be that person again and this is where a strong will is needed to let the appearance of their old self fade away and embrace this new person by continuing their fight against cancer so they can experience a new life with a new countenance.

It takes a positive mental attitude from the patient as well as those providing support to the patient to help them battle cancer and recover from surgery, chemotherapy, and radiation. An understanding by supporters that their care, concern and assistance is a medicine that in combination with the cancer treatments can bring about healing from the disease. By carrying on a normal life as possible and staying in contact with family and friends, a powerful source of life is provided that will uplift the patient during their lowest times and make them very optimistic about their future.

Feeling ill and listless from chemotherapy and radiation cannot be avoided no matter the best intentions of doctors and the greatest of care from medical personnel, family, and friends. Through preparation, anticipation, and endurance, a patient can survive the sickness of it all. The patient has to deal with the disease using all of their abilities but they must not give it any power over their future because the purpose of life is to live it and overcome adversities and obstacles that inhibit one's path. The cancer and the illness may last a few years but the joy of living will last a lifetime.

Posted 04/27/2017

SUMMATION. The effects of chemotherapy and radiation on the body is devastating and takes months and even years for the body to recover. Although, recent forms of chemotherapy are not as harsh as in the past. There are medications that can lessen the severity of chemotherapy and maintaining a proper high protein diet can help the body battle the cancer and also the effects of the chemotherapy and radiation. These two forms of treatment are able to fight cancer but the patient has to endure complications that they are unable to survive. Some patients decide to use only one form of these treatments rather than having both forms of care administered to their body and enduring painful and nauseating stress.

There are alternative methods for cancer treatment but oftentimes they are not offered to patients. Doctors and hospitals operate in networks which have relationships with drug and pharmaceutical companies and will only offer the patient a form of treatment using drugs manufactured by these companies. Some doctors are not aware of new forms of cancer treatment and only offer a cancer patient a form of treatment that is known to them and issued routinely. It is important that a patient and their family do research on cancer treatments because there are other methods beside chemotherapy and radiation. The health of seriously ill people is not as important as the bottom line of drug and pharmaceutical companies. New methods of treatment are available but are possibly being blocked by these companies to prevent their drugs from becoming rarely used and unable to make them profits. There is no recurring profit in a medical cure as there is in a medical drug that helps a person stay alive so people will continue to suffer, some will die as long as health care is seen as a business and not as method to sustain life.

Their Music Plays On
(When Musical Artists Pass Away)

Song is an experience that is carried by a person through all stages of their life. It may begin with a mother singing to her unborn child, a lullaby sung by a father as he puts his child to bed, or a playful melody from a child's toy. These are initial introductions to music that many will never forget and will be reflected upon at certain times the rest of their lives. As the person ages, they will choose style type, and genre of music which is their favorite to enjoy. This usually leads to the person selecting artists who performs their favorite form of music as entertainers whose careers they will follow.

An attachment is developed between the person and the artists of their favorite music though, they have never met the artists or watched them perform in person at a concert. The bond is connected by nights of the person falling asleep to the music of the artists, listening to the music while doing work around the house, or preparing dinner to the music. During the most private moments, it is the music of the artists that brings comfort to the person who may be experiencing loss as in the death of a parent, relative, or friend, a disagreement or breakup with a girlfriend, boyfriend, or friend, or losing a large sum of money or job. An inspiration may be derived from the music of the artists by the person that causes them to write, play a musical instrument, or act, helps them create a great work of art, or erodes their doubts and fears so they can fulfill their dreams. It is the artists who shows understanding and through their music provides a friendship that helps the person deal with situations in life.

A sudden death at an early age by a musical artist is as devastating as a family member or close friend to a person who followed their career but never knew them personally. They knew them through their music and have shared with them the most intimate moments and personal experiences. Listening to their music, the person can recall every detail of their fondest day, every tear shed on their saddest day, and the joy they felt an their best day. The person is distraught that someone from their past has left them so early and they did not have a chance to say goodbye or have the opportunity to share one last song together.

There will be celebrations and honors to commemorate the tragic loss of the musical artist with radio stations constantly playing their hits and many television shows giving recognition as well as the news periodically inserting segments that give a brief biography of the musical artist. It is wonderful that the musical artist is receiving acknowledgment and accolades on a fabulous career but those with a personal musical attachment will feel a great life expired too soon and the songs that brought so much expression to life now bring a finality. This moment can be equated to hearing great music as a youth and discovering the musical artist had passed away years earlier and the thought of how great it would be if they were still alive comes to mind every time their music is heard. Now, the person will have the same feeling when they hear the music of their departed musical artist.

After a year or more has passed, unreleased songs will be made available to the public but they will not have the finishing touches of the musical artist that made their music special and familiar to the loyal fan that has known their great music as the soundtrack of their lives. Styles changed, times changed and the person and the musical artist went through the changes together but this time the person will have to go through the change alone. The music the musical artist has provided to overcome adversity and sadness in the past will now have to be used by the person to get over the tragic loss of one of their favorite artist. Their music plays on and will forever without any new memories being created from new music but now the old music is a lot more special.

Posted 04/30/2017

SUMMATION.   Their music, their songs, their sound are musical pyramids that will last longer than they lived on Earth and be enjoyed by generations they will never know but have provided them with inspiration. A favorite artist (known as a legend, an icon, one of the greatest of all times) has left such a magnificent musical impression while on this Earth that for their fans and all who have heard their music, it is hard to imagine a decade without hearing their songs. However, to understand their greatness and importance to the world, imagine if they never existed and no one had been able to hear this music, their songs, their sound.

Fans are stunned at the lost of their favorite artists with a sudden grief in the manner of losing a family member even though they may have never been physically introduced to their favorite artists, they have grown to know them through the music which has been there with the fan during their great moments and bad experiences. Now, when they reminisce about these times they will also think of the artists. A friend from a distance who they followed and kept up with more than their own relatives. Movies will mark history with the the music of the artists by using it in scenes and soundtracks that introduce their songs to a younger audience and will inspire new artists to create from their sound. No, they are unable to perform any longer but their music will play on.

Using A Broad Stroke
(Grouping People of Color)

The land that would eventually become America was unknown to most of the world until Christopher Columbus arrived on his voyage from Spain. He would return to claim the land for King Ferdinand and Queen Isabella though, there were people already inhabiting this new land who he would call Indians because he thought he was in Asia. This name would be attached to all of these people of this new land by people of the *Old Country* who would enter this land as immigrants with the belief that all of the inhabitants of the *New World* with the same complexion were Indians despite their differences in language, dress, and way of life.

The people who were called Indians, now known as Native-Americans, were members of different tribes who had their own culture but were all mixed together with a broad stroke by the immigrants so it would be easy and they could feel guiltless about invading and killing the people to cleanse the land of the tribes to take land. By overpowering the tribes, they were able to reduce the use of their languages and almost eradicate their cultures. There was never any repudiation for being called Indians and Native-Americans by the native peoples as primitive beliefs and discrimination were allowed to persist that the few surviving tribes are living on reservations but have never returned to the multitude of their ancestors that thrived on the land before the colonial immigrants arrived.

A similar experience was suffered by the people called Africans who were removed from their land and forced into slavery. It was opportunists who went to the land they called the *Dark Continent* and blended these people together by calling them Africans. This made it easy and acceptable to start the institution of slavery and disconnect these groups of people from their culture, language, and land that they have no reverence to their ancestors. Using a broad stroke, the African name was forced on the people of Africa by their oppressors and their descendants have formed an allegiance to the country they are in which has continued the derogatory perceptions of their persecutors while the descendants have never interceded to stop the usage and demand to use a name of their own.

In the 2016 Presidential Election, a major issue was illegal immigrants coming across the southern border of the United States. Many American citizens consider the people to be citizens of Mexico because most of them speak the Spanish language. Using a broad stroke, the people seeking opportunity in an attempt to make a better a life for themselves and their families were grouped together by some Americans who do not realize several of these people come from beyond the borders of Mexico with different cultures but must pass through the country to get to the United States. However, the brush is not used upon illegal immigrants who cross the northern border of the United States. This stigma is placed on a people who are fearful of being deported if they choose to speak out to change it.

Grouping people of color with names that are not highly regarded or prestigious and consist of negative connotations is a way to separate those of power and privilege from people who are different and not welcomed. A method for restricting a people without using imprisonment or slavery is to give them a derogatory name that is a burden not only for them but it will also be an impediment for their future generations. Words are only powerful according to the understanding and response of the listener. However, a name can pave a smooth road in life for some and a life of rough roads and long journeys for others. Until people take hold of the brush to make their own name, they will continue to be at the mercy of those holding the brush. A name gains power when someone answers to it and accepts it as their own.

Posted 05/05/2017

SUMMATION.   A fact that America is yet to acknowledge is that Black people were on the continent before the first pilgrims arrived. The story written into history is the people met Christopher Columbus and the pilgrims were proclaimed to be Indians by the foreigners. However, there is no admittance of this by America as it is told that Black Americans are the descendants of African people. This was possibly done as an excuse not to give Black Americans land as was given Native-Americans. Nor do Blacks receive any benefits or funds for having their land taken as do Native-Americans. Black Americans are descendants of Black slaves, this is not totally true as this story may have been told to hide the intelligence of Black people to make them appear to be inferior human beings and the fact that Africans had been crossing the Atlantic years before Europeans.

Colonists invaded the lands of native people and named the group of people primarily because they could not speak their language. It is an assertion that the colonists came up with the names that is why the term *"Black"* and *"White"* are capitalized in these posts. With one large stroke of a brush, different groups of people in their own environment were painted together, even though they were not related, because of how they looked while their culture, language, and centuries of living on their land before ever seeing colonists were ignored. Some people accept the name and try to fit into the group they are associated with never realizing they will always be seen as inferior. Selecting their own name and identifying themselves gives them the ability to be who they want to be and not the caricatures and stereotypes placed on them by colonists.

The Last Stand
(Sears)

An American classic is struggling to remain in business as its retail sales are so low it is closer to going out of business than recovering and being an industry leader once again. At one time, Sears was the favorite store of many American families to do their shopping as it had departments that gratified moms, dads, and children while items were made purchasable for customers by use of cash, credit, or layaway plans. It also was a model for other companies who wanted to copy the success it had been able to maintain over the years.

One of the best marketing strategies to be implemented in business was used by Sears. The issuance of catalogs by Sears was a lucrative marketing concept that not only gave people the opportunity to order by mail or by telephone but it was also free advertising as the catalog could be seen in most homes and business offices. Sears delighted many people with its Christmas edition as customers were able to look at many items on the pages of the big book and children ran home with it from the mailbox to make their wish lists to send to Santa Claus.

In the beginning, the company was known as Sears, Roebuck, and Company after its founders Richard W. Sears and Alvin C. Roebuck who started the business after Sears received a box of watches by error. He would start selling watches and jewelry and hire Roebuck who was a watch repairman and eventually became his partner. It started as a mail ordering catalog company in 1886 and based in Chicago and would open stores in 1925. The company gained notoriety by providing quality products at moderate prices that farmers could afford. Sears and Roebuck flourished when it began operating retail locations in heavily populated urban cities while continuing to serve their rural customers by use of their catalog. Sears would construct the tallest building in the world at the time in 1974. The 110-story Sears Tower would take the aforementioned title away from the World Trade Center in New York City.

Major national brands would be established by the company who reduced its name to Sears as customers formed an attachment to their products. Most carpenters, handymen, and auto mechanics preferred *Craftsman* tools to perform their job tasks at home and at work. *Kenmore* appliances were desired in the home by many couples who were impressed by the longevity of the products. Moms dressed their boys in *Toughskins* jeans because of their durability to last beyond a school year. Dads along with their sons could be seen on any summer Saturday replacing their car batter with a *Diehard* battery because of its quality and replacement warranty.

As more stores opened and the company faced new retail competition, the luster of the big catalog wore off as customers enjoyed going to stores to see the products rather than looking at the pages. Then, the invention of the Internet enabled some companies to sell their products online which many customers found as a convenience as it saved them a trip to stores that were in overcrowded malls with hard-to-find parking that seemed a mile from the store. This is an updated version of a catalog ordering company concept that Sears had used and it caused several companies to go out of business. The Sears catalog had been surpassed as it could only be obtained at request with a $5 fee.

In 2004, Sears would be acquired by Kmart but

it has not provided any improvement in the business as the company continues store closings. The last stand for Sears could be to only operate a few retail stores and return to the use of their catalog by creating an app that is available for American consumers while expanding to customers worldwide. As companies copied their business strategy in the past, it may be time for Sears to copy the concept of a company like Amazon. This may be for naught as Sears nears the end because there are few customers who remember the acclaim of this great company and feeling the excitement of opening the mailbox and receiving a Sears catalog.

Posted 05/24/2017

SUMMATION.   Sears, Kmart, and ToysRUs are making their way into American nostalgia along with malls and other retail stores. The curiosity and delight of walking through a store of new clothes, products, and items is of past generations. It is a new day when all of the stores and products are at hand on a phone or computer and can be delivered to the front door. No need to spend money on gas, fight traffic, and not find that particular item after walking around a store or mall for a couple of hours. There are some who still like to walk through the glass doors, they are probably the same people who miss Blockbuster Video, Circuit City, and pay telephones out on the street.

Home is becoming the new place to shop in today's society. A shopper can order a new car from their bed and have it delivered to their driveway; a family meal for each day of the week and groceries can be delivered to the home or ready for pick up at the store; new movies that are at the theaters can be seen by a person in their home theater. The Internet has replaced the catalogs from Sears that a shopper would receive each season. There are more items and the customer can shop around for the best deal and lowest price. While the customers who have known Sears, malls, and other popular retail stores will miss them when they close, they are like TV antennas, videocassettes, CD's to a younger generation . . . only a thing of the past.

Death Is Always Untimely
(The Serengeti, Sandy Hook,
Virginia Tech)

The Serengeti is where a magnificent migration takes place from northern Tanzania to southwestern Kenya covering 12,000 square miles of Africa. Wildebeests, gazelles, and zebras are among the animals that are a part of this natural phenomena each year. By instinct, intellect, and congenital traits, the journey is made with the animals knowing that all of them will not reach their destination due to thirst, hunger, exhaustion, or predation. In attempting to cross the Grumeti and Mara Rivers, the animals have to battle the rushing waters with the threat of being attacked by crocodiles. Many will face death at these points but the animals will continue on with the migration.

Knowing the dangers and that deaths will occur during their journey does not alleviate the pain of loss for the animals. There are times crocodiles will die during a struggle but their grief is never seen because they are under water and sometimes will eat their own. Among the migratory animals, a mother may search for her young one until she can wait no longer or a calf may cry out for its mother before it must move along with the group to prevent being susceptible to predators. Their is a sadness in their eyes and despair is easy to recognize by their reluctance to go on as they linger in hope of their missing member. Although death is expected, it seems they were not prepared for it on such a strenuous trip. The untimely loss to their family leaves them bewildered and longing to have their member running along side of them as they continue on their journey.

People have a common practice that starts in the fall and ends during the spring. Rising early every Monday through Friday, parents take their children to school to be educated with the expectation of picking them up or seeing them at home later on in the day. On the last morning of the school week in Newtown, CT, the routines for parents, students, faculty and staff would forever be interrupted. Sandy Hook Elementary School would bring the Nation to sorrow from experiencing a tragic shooting that took the lives of 26 people. The gunman was a 20-year old man who donned combat gear and presented semiautomatic pistols and a semiautomatic rifle that he fired to kill a total of 20 children.

Parents returned to the school hours earlier than their usual pickup time due to the tragedy anxiously looking for their children. Many students were able to find their parents who were thankful and greeted them with a hug before rushing them away to the safety of their home. Then there were these parents who waited with sadness in their eyes and their despair was easy to notice as they watch other relieved parents rushed past them with their children. Schools are a safe place for children where parents only fear illnesses or minor injuries but the untimely loss for these parents left them bewildered and longing to have their children run into their arms so the could hurry to the safety of their homes.

Sending a child to college fills a parent with pride but also trepidation as their gains of knowledge and valuable life experiences does not ease the concern of the parent who can no longer keep them safe. On April 16, 2007, a lone gunmen opened fire on the campus of Virginia Tech killing 32 people and causing wounds to 17 others in two separate attacks. This reprehensible act not only shocked the Nation, it brought fear to parents who were unable to provide protection for their children miles away at college. These violent acts have made parents realize that some children who go off to school and college may not return home despite their best intentions and preparedness for their children.

The two men who committed these violent attacks chose their victims randomly before they turned their guns on the persons who caused them the most problems, themselves. These perpetrators are the crocodiles who prevented other students and faculty from continuing on their way through their journey of life. Their parents and relatives receded to their homes and traveled in the shadows, not in support of their family member or condoning their criminal acts but for the grief and loss of the families and the shame that is unfortunately and undeservedly brought on the family. Loss of life can happen at any time still, death is always untimely and those effected will long for their love one as they reluctantly stagger on their way.

Posted 05/28/2017

SUMMATION. Schools and colleges, shopping malls and concerts are where children gather and the major concern of parents is that their children will make it to their destination safely and back home without any problems. Today, parents have a greater concern as school shootings, mass shootings, and mall shootings are becoming common occurrences that are taking the lives of many children. Students are taking the initiative to protest against state and federal governments for gun law reform and school safety however, most school shootings are carried out by a classmate. It is possible the problem is not being noticed by parents, faculty, and students of why this child has resorted to taking this violent action.

Hurt people usually hurt the people that are close to them and the people who are in and around the places they frequent. On some occasions they are apprehended and taken to jail but most of the time they will take their own life after taking the lives of innocent people. All because they had a problem that they did not know how to deal with it and was not comfortable asking someone for help. Parents have to teach their children to be observant of all people wherever they go and aware of their surroundings. This also includes while driving in case they are being followed. It is best to be cautious and look for danger than to become a shooting victim who does not return home to their parents.

Celebrity Does Not Prevent Tragedy
(The Rich and Famous)

The arrest of Tiger Woods saddened many people who are awaiting for him to return to his championship form in golf. They were disheartened to see their favorite golfer in a delusional state captured in a video and a mug shot that is embarrassing and humiliating. A great player and ambassador of golf has fallen on hard times due to family hardships and injuries that have disrupted his game and now many people believe he has descended to a depth so low that there may not be a chance of recovery. Common, everyday people place celebrities on such a high pedestal that it is unreasonable to expect someone to maintain a balance life through the ups and downs of maturing into an adult, being a spouse, learning to be a parent, and experiencing death.

Tiger's arrest was a major news story that is still being discussed on TV shows and finding space in print magazines and newspapers while being passed to friends through social media. It is a topic of conversation in small towns and cities just as it is in large metropolitan areas. An arrest of a celebrity is breaking news but if most people look in their local newspaper they can read about a similar arrest of normal citizens daily or weekly that does not make the news outside of their area. There are papers that only report on people being arrested that are positioned on counters or near the entrance of convenience stores but many customers glance at them and walk out of the store without purchasing one. For most people breaking the law is more interesting when someone rich and famous is involved.

Reading about an embarrassing moment or compromising position that a person of popularity has experienced is the highlight of some people's day. There seems to be a comfort in seeing someone rich and famous falter which gives the impression that some people believe prosperous individuals are treacherous and vindictive and get all the breaks while common people are hard-working and virtuous and cannot have a luck of good fortune. These are misconceptions that consume some people because they are unhappy with their lives or they find their life uninteresting so they live their life through a person with popularity or they want to see someone famous experience adversity comparable to or worse than common people.

Many rich and famous people live their life on a public stage whether they want to or not. Those who seek privacy often have it infringed upon without any regard nor respect of being with their family. The people who get a thrill out of a celebrity being arrested are the same people who get enjoyment at a peek of a celebrity during a private moment. There is never any thought given to their reaction due to their privacy being interrupted and interfered with during a special moment in their life with a spouse, a child, or family member that was planned and is now ruined. Anonymity is loss when celebrity and fame is gained but is often longed for when trying to live a normal life.

Being a celebrity does not prevent tragedy but in spite of the shocking event the celebrity will have the means to recover from their unfortunate situation. Most celebrities move forward and live a life better than those who reported on their story and all of the people who read about it. Life for the rich and famous is financially superlative to that of a common person but they will face adversity also but it will be more publicized. It is easy and quick to go from famous to infamous as an indiscretion of a celebrity will be past online and sent around the world in a second and talked about on TV for days possibly weeks where the faults of a common person will only be found in the local newspaper and in that paper that sits on the counter or near the entrance of convenience stores.

Posted 06/01/2017

SUMMATION.   The golf world is excited to see Tiger Woods playing competitive golf again. Renewed interest by fans who were drawn to the game by Tiger are happy he is bringing the sport back to relevancy. After suffering an humiliating fall from grace, Tiger is gaining the support of many golfers, fans, and analysts who were appalled and disappointed by his behavior. These are some of the same people who ridiculed and piled on the golfer while he was down and trying to gain his footing in life. He struggled with addiction to prescription drugs while recovering from surgeries and trying to return to his championship form before the world. A humble Tiger changed his attitude and manner on the golf course and attitudes of the fans changed about the golfer.

People love the story of the underdog. It is what makes David and Goliath one of the most well-known stories of the Bible. The U.S. Hockey team defeating Russia for the gold medal in the 1980 Winter Olympics is a phenomenal story. However, people are also fascinated with a person rising to popularity and fame only to experience a tragic descend publicly then gather themselves to have success again. It is the fault of those who become rich and famous and then take an embarrassing plummet because they ignore the examples before them or do not learn of them and go down the same road. Popularity and riches blinds them into believing they have unlimited privileges only to learn it is a harder landing to the ground from high upon a pedestal than tumbling to the earth from making a misstep while walking.

And The Home of The Depraved
(The Land of The Free)

It is the American dream. Once it was a husband with a good job buying a beautiful home with a yard enclosed by a white picket fence for his wife and children but now it is a husband and wife with good jobs buying a beautiful home in a safe neighborhood in a district with a great schools for their children. A neighborhood with all White residents was considered ideal and enticing to other ethnic groups, especially Blacks who wanted a better life for their families and a better education for their children even if it meant living among a group of people who did not consider them welcomed. For some Black people, this significant matter was worth the trouble rather than being disenfranchised and not represented living with their own people.

However, this American dream was made difficult to achieve for Black folks as homes in these neighborhoods were not offered to Black families or banks would not grant them loans for homes in these areas. A practice called *"redlining"* was used to keep Black people in Black neighborhoods or lower class mixed neighborhoods by banks offering them loans on houses in these communities. Some Black families prevailed in spite of the practice and moved into White communities but they endured harassment and threats in their *ideal* neighborhood. A rock or hard object was thrown to break out a window in their home and racial slurs and threat would be painted on their house. Part of their fence would be damaged and a cross would be burned in their yard.

Neighborhoods have become diverse but it was through the passage of laws not from people accepting a different group of people. Blacks with notoriety are facing harassment the same as Black veterans returning from fighting in World War II. They returned to America decorated and victorious soldiers but were still not welcomed in White neighborhoods. Today, Blacks may pay more for a house than White residents in a prominent neighborhood at a higher interest rate even after submitting a substantial down payment. The police will follow them through their neighborhood to their residence regularly despite knowing the Black family is living in the home.

LeBron James has learned that being the best basketball player in the world, a champion, appearing in commercials, and being wealthy does not prevent him from experiencing racism. In the city of Brentwood, CA, vandals defiled his home by painting a racial slur on the dwelling. While many people were shocked and appalled and some Blacks were angered by the act, most Blacks have the understanding that it does not matter the level of education attained, success achieved, or wealth gained as it will not alleviate racism because regardless of the improvement, the appearance of being Black has not been removed. There is no achievement that can remove the importance of being Black nor should any Black person want it removed because they did not reach their accomplishment in spite of their Black nature but it was their Black nature that made them great.

A belief by Black people that the *"White man's ice is colder"* meaning everything White-owned or managed by Whites is better has to end. Blacks are so determined to run away from their home among the lions and let it become devalued to settle in a place they believe is paradise only to find out it is inhabited with snakes. It is time for Blacks to make a correction by improving and building new neighborhoods and also improving themselves instead of continuing to leave their communities to live among people who would be happier to see them go than to have them stay. A successful community by Blacks is possible if they make a commitment to build it so they can live in the land of the free instead of the home of the depraved and relinquish the belief that life is better among people who do no want them in their neighborhood.

Posted 06/07/2017

SUMMATION. It is useless to try to force people who do not want to live next to each other to try to be civil and neighborly in a community developed for diversity. In the past, laws were passed and unwritten rules were followed to keep certain groups away from groups who mostly populated they state, the city, and the neighborhoods. The reason these laws and unsaid codes were successful at keeping certain groups out of particular neighborhoods is the people who heavily populated the community made sure they were followed while the police and public officials backed them up by enforcing the law. Many cities and towns are divided by railroad tracks with disenfranchised groups on the side that is neglected and prominent groups are on the side that receives the most taxes and public services.

At one time in America, Whites had no problem living with and next to Blacks. During slavery, Whites had Blacks in their homes working and even had rooms where they allowed Black slaves to live so they could be close by when needed. Most of the Black slaves lived in quarters on the plantation so they would be near their work. However, once slavery was abolished Whites did not want to live next to Blacks and hated their existence. Blacks have to realize that the more they strive and exercise their equal rights, they will continue to face resentment from Whites who have every intention to push them back *"in their place."* Blacks will never change the attitudes of most Whites so they must develop a mindset that there is no better place than their own.

Private Thoughts and Conversations
(Said Out Loud)

During the football pregame show, *The NFL Today,* a statement was made by one of the co-hosts of the show that shocked and offended its American audience in 1988. Shocking, because it was said publicly and on national television. Offensive, because it declared one race of people was more dominant over all other races in sports due to a deplorable act in world history. In speaking about the greatness of Black athletes, Jimmy *"The Greek"* Snyder stated their physical prowess was the result of *"specialized"* breeding during slavery. The strongest and tolerable Black female slave was mated with the most powerful and potent Black male slave to produce *"superior"* slaves.

There is some truth in what Jimmy *"The Greek"* said as slave masters did breed their most prominent Black male and female slaves with each other for better workers and servants and to produce their own slaves so they did not have to buy more from slave traders. Breeding farms were also established and continued far after the Trans-Atlantic Slave Trade ended. However, the remark revisited a past that many did not want to acknowledge or the subject explored while making the *"superior"* White race unequaled to the *"inferior"* Black race. Although responses to Snyder's comment were mixed, he was removed from the show and never seen on national TV again.

Comedians evolved from the jesters who held court to make people laugh and entertain Kings and Queens. They were usually the only ones among the townspeople who could make jokes about the King and

Queen and not face retribution. Although, there were times when the jester may go too far or not be entertaining and be removed from performing, locked in a dungeon, or put to death. Comedienne Kathy Griffin made a video with her holding a mock decapitated head of President Donald Trump that was drenched in fake blood. She was immediately lambasted at her disgusting attempt at humor. What Griffin failed to take in consideration was that she was not only disrespecting Trump who is the President but more importantly, she was disrespecting the Office of the President of the United States. This is what people, even Trump opponents, found reprehensible. Griffin has been dismissed by CNN and has had to cancel concert tour dates.

While interviewing Senator Ben Sasse of Nebraska, Bill Maher blurted out a response that shocked some people and irritated others. Senator Sasse offered an invitation to Maher to come work in the field with him and other Nebraskans when Maher (with hands raised) delivered, *"I'm a house nigga!"* in an attempt at humor. Quickly, people responded because they were shocked he would be insensitive to a horrible experience for the ancestors of Black people. It also bothered Black people that he felt so comfortable in using the derogatory description so freely. Maher made a prompt apology realizing he was unintentionally contributing to the rising volatile racial climate that has emerged and been embolden under the new President and his administration. HBO has not removed *Real Time With Bill Maher* from its programming nor has it reprimanded Maher. It is unknown if there has been a reduction in HBO subscribers in objection.

Many people find these acts appalling and disruptive to any prospects of racial harmony and respect. However, there are some who are not stunned by the acts or words but displeased they were said out loud for these are private thoughts one holds in secrecy or are said in private conversation among people with similar beliefs. When people are forced to act in a certain manner publicly, they choose to be themselves privately. In these new times, old ways have been intentionally shown openly by those in power to disrespect those they consider inferior. While racial slurs and derogatory acts distract the masses, the wealthy make laws and abuse power to increase their riches and exert their will on the lower classes.

Posted 06/19/2017

SUMMATION.   The opportunity to speak to a mass audience should be taken with a responsibility to be informative and entertaining to viewers who listen attentively to their words. Some feel they have to say outlandish things to maintain their audience while others become embolden by their popularity and believe they can say whatever comes to their mind. Their audience has grown, the ratings of their show is high, and they are in demand to appear on other shows. They continue to push the envelope by making strong comments or insensitive remarks on controversial topics and receive support from a large segment of their audience. This is until they make a comment that some find offensive although their core fans will give them support, it is their employer and advertisers who will have to make a decision on the comments because it does not conform to their standards.

Ramifications can significantly damage careers as in the cases of Jimmy *"The Greek"* Snyder, comedians Kathy Griffin and Michael Richards (who used the n-word during his stand-up act in a comedy club) and prevent them form regaining their successful status and popularity. Meanwhile, President Donald Trump and Bill Maher faced no retribution and continue to prosper. It can be learned from these situations that the person's likability can absolve them of their strong or offensive comments. Roseanne Barr was dismissed from her top-rated sitcom *"Roseanne"* for sending a racist tweet, Mel Gibson's career has faltered after going on a rant laced with racial slurs while former President Bill Clinton is revered after lying about his illicit liaison with Monica Lewinsky and Paula Deen has revived her career after losing her cooking show for making a racial slur. This is the era of social media where anyone can comment on any topic and the door has been opened on private conversations. There will be more public figures who take the chance on making unfiltered comments and suffer the consequences.

A Revolution
Cannot Be Lead From The Grave
(Faux Power In Death)

They spoke powerful words when they delivered stirring messages and showed phenomenal courage by taking unpopular stands for their people. In the struggle, constant opposition came from those who vehemently despised them and many of their own people who did not agree with their actions. However, in death they are celebrated because they are no longer a threat to an oppressive system and now, they are held up on high in front of their people and shown respect by those who used to oppose them but it is actually to keep their people calm and *in their place*. Younger generations learn of their words, try to revive their messages and show courage by speaking out however, they are only repeating their words and not adding to the messages a modern strategy that can uplift their people out of *their place*.

There have been Black people who have spoken out on the injustices experienced by Black people and led movements for Black people to have equal rights, civil rights, and human rights however, they were denounced and met with opposition by those who refused and were unwilling to improve conditions for Black people. People who had the means to use military and legal resources and terrorist acts attacked and assaulted Black leaders and activists because their words were so potent and their messages influenced their people to organize, mobilize, and determined to fight for their rights. This caused fear to those who wanted to keep a system in place that gave them power and privilege and continued to oppress Black people.

An attack on the character of Black leaders and advocates who aimed to achieve rights for their people was done by their opposition through newspapers, radio, and television to influence public opinion and to create anger against Black activists. By demonizing Black activists, their potent words were not able to be heard and their messages understood because of the resentment built up from those in support of an oppressive system. This caused a discord among Black people. There have been Black people given a platform and resources to speak against Black activists to cause divisiveness and confusion among Black people so a movement would be quelled and disassembled. The great Black leaders were removed from leading organizations which resulted in Black groups settling on resolutions that fell far below their objectives.

After these impeccable Black leaders were quieted by death (usually assassination) or imprisonment, their words and their messages have been misconstrued so they can be structured to control and direct the masses of Black people to accept and participate in a system that benefits those of power and privilege while belittling and confusing those who are underrepresented while keeping them fearful and in a condition of struggle. There will be monuments and statues made honoring Black leaders and activists, exhibits will be displayed in museums, literature about their works and speeches will be published, and documentaries about their life will be produced to give Black people pride and show them images of courage to convince them to assimilate into the system.

Black leaders of the past are being studied and their messages are resonating with a young Black generation who are finding their words are still potent and relevant as they address the issues and problems of today. This has inspired many young Black activists to speak out courageously and bring awareness to their people. However, some try to use the Black leaders to start a movement from the grave because of the historical relevance of their name and the manner in which they made the world pay attention to their issues and demanded that those in power listen. Their time has past and it is time for new voices to bring the messages in a new way. By continuing to place former Black leaders out in front of their campaign for social change causes Black people to reflect on the past when they are presently in the midst of turmoil.

Some Black leaders of the past have been given faux power in death which has diluted the potency of their words and distorted their messages that have become acceptable to a lot more people than in the past when people got offended. The revolution, a movement, has to be orchestrated by Black leaders who are alive with an understanding in the knowledge held by Black leaders and Black scholars of the past to bring about equal rights, civil rights, and human rights for their people. Black people cannot be distracted by their oppressors who hold Black leaders of the past up in the light because it is only to blind them from the Black leaders' true plight.

Posted 06/29/2017

SUMMATION. Black leaders and activists of the past are now being quoted and referenced by people who are not Black because their words are inspiring, potent, and still relevant. However, they are often misquoted and taken out of context to push back against young Black activists in an attempt to make them believe they are disrespecting these great Black leaders and activists of the past who sacrificed, struggle, and died trying to change the condition and future for their people. Now that new Black groups are emerging, non-Black people and some Black people are using the words and glorifying the actions of Black leaders and activists of the past in a defiant reaction against the growing activism of a young Black generation intent on removing old and outdated social standards.

Young Black activists and new Black groups are critically compared to Black leaders and Black groups of the past, specifically by opposition and older Blacks who want them to be structured and have the character of Black organizations of the past. The words of these Black leaders and activists can be used for instruction and their actions to unite Black people. They have ran their leg of the race and young Black activists and new Black groups have to take up the baton and continue the race in their own manner with new strategies and a greater sense of urgency to hand off the baton to the next generation in a condition for them to have a chance of pulling ahead in the race. Using the old methods will only provide the same results which will keep Blacks *"in their place."*

It Is Hard To Tell
(Black Lives Matter)

During the Civil Rights Movement, Black people cold be heard singing *"We Shall Overcome"* and chanting *"Black Power!"* and demanding *"Power To The People!"* as Black men were wearing white signs with black letters that read: *"I Am A Man" as* they demonstrated. This was to show unity and determination to change the condition of Black people in America and that they would continue to move forward and not be turned around because they were filled with conviction to attain their civil rights, their equal rights, and their human rights in a country that had only considered them property. They sacrificed their time by working tirelessly, organizing, and protesting, their freedom by being arrested and sent to jail, and their lives by confronting those who believed and participated in furthering their oppression that they would lynch or shoot to kill them then bury their bodies in a hidden grave or sink them in a small pond or obscure area of a lake.

The modern Black generation has new words that have reverberated around the world. They chant *"Black Lives Matter"* when they march and have it printed in black letters on white signs to bring attention to and demand the stoppage of the police killing Black people, many who were unarmed and had not committed a crime. These words started online via social media where they spread and became so potent that they jumped out of cyberworld into the real world with such velocity it was called a movement by opposition before it was truly organized. In order to dilute the strength of the words, some people tried to change the first word to give their cause significance. *"All Lives Matter," "White Lives Matter,"* and *"Blue Lives Matter"* amplified by news media but they never gained the power of *"Black Lives Matter"* as they only reminded people of the original concept.

The push back that has been difficult to refute by the Black Lives Matter group is the continued murders of Black people by Black people. A common response by many Black people is that people commit crimes against those who are within proximity of their community. This is true however, an awareness by Black people has to materialize so it can be known that if Black people are killing Black people and the police are killing Black people, the destruction of their people is being caused by the reduction of their people. Having a segment of the population murdered, a segment incarcerated, a portion uneducated, and a portion unemployed weakens a people and makes them incapable of improving their condition and causes them to be susceptible to a systemic structure that keeps them *"in their place"* and to gentrification where they can be moved without regard by those in power.

Black people are not cleaning their homes and keeping up the maintenance on their lawns but are expecting others to show concern and provide support. It is imperative that Black lives matter to Black people because they are beneficial to other people. They provide residual income and generational wealth for others while owning very little in life and lacking any significance to pass on to the next generation. A Black life has to become too valuable to be taken so easily by Black people and too important to be allowed to be taken by others. The life of a Black person is being taken every other day or every week by the police and others because Black people are waiting to be shown care and respect but are not displaying it to each other. *"Black Lives Matter"* will be synonymous with this Black generation but when it is researched by others in the future it will be hard to tell how a Black life was appreciated by Black people because of the Black death that persisted at the hands of their own people.

Posted 07/14/2017

SUMMATION.   A Black life was disrespected and demeaned with the inception of slavery. Slave traders and slave owners treated Blacks as a commodity and as property. Their brutal and inhumane treatment of Blacks was forced on Black slaves to control and teach to other Black slaves to maintain order on plantations and to keep Blacks *"in their place."* This cruel and reprehensible behavior was copied and taken on by Blacks. After slavery ended, Blacks were devalued and brutality toward them escalated. The savagery was not limited to Whites as some Blacks acted violently toward other Blacks because they were no longer protected by a slave owner and they had very little protection under the law.

Blacks are still enduring cruelty from their own people but are reluctant to bring the same outrage to Black criminals as they do police officers and White people who perpetrate violence against Black people. Black activists and Black groups proclaim their love for their people by fighting to change laws and improve their condition but they remain silent about the Black criminality that is prevalent in the Black community and among Black people. A high Black crime rate is present in Black cities with Black mayors and Black responsibility is low. It cannot be rationalized for other people to care about Black lives when Black people do not care about Black lives.

The Forgotten People

(Mental Illness)

Once upon a time in America, families were protective and secretive about family members who were afflicted with mental illness and physical disabilities. They would stay in the back of the house in a bedroom or downstairs in the basement or possibly upstairs in the attic. Visitors may not realize they were in the house unless they were acquainted with them and would go back for a visit if allowed by the family. On occasions, they may have been taken out with the family during shopping and dress up to attend church but most of the time they resided at home. This could have been from shame by the family or from a standpoint of manageability as it was easier for them to be their caretaker at home than out among the public. For some, it was too much to be a caretaker of the mentally disabled and they had their family members admitted to mental hospitals and institutions.

Facilities that specialized in care for those with mental afflictions were a great help to families who were unable to provide care for their family members. Most of these hospitals and institutions were funded by state governments and were beneficial to families who could not afford private facilities. In recent years, state governments have closed most of these hospitals and institutions which caused many of the residents to be released back to their family members who may be too old to care for them or to unacquainted family members because known relatives have passed on. Death of family members have caused many of these former patients to become homeless and living on the streets. They are passed by and looked upon as hideous sites among many in society but there are some who provide aid by giving them money, clothes, and food of which state governments could have continued to provide assistance and support for people who are mentally troubled.

Adding to the homeless population who are mentally ill are military veterans returning home from tours, more often several and consecutive tours, in war torn areas around the world. The United States government have failed to provide care and support to soldiers who have fulfilled their obligation to their country and now need help for their problems caused by being in conflicts and battles just as state governments stop providing care and support for their mentally ill citizens. Instead of receiving the proper medical attention, many are self-medicating with street drugs which are making their problems more adverse and causing them to be a danger to themselves and others. Some will be arrested and jailed and receive some medical attention but will soon be released back into society that does not acknowledgment their illness.

These forgotten people are not showed any attention until they commit a violent act or crime. Many recent shootings where people were killed have been committed by people who had mental problems. The apathetic behavior of the federal and state governments to ignore people with a mental illness has caused significant problems. Unable to receive even minor treatment, people with mental illness are finding it difficult to deal with American society that is forever changing and is just as challenging for common citizens. Violent outbursts and criminal acts will continue as long as people are not receiving the medical attention they need and self-medicating with inappropriate drugs. America has to decide to take care of its forgotten people or they will continue to make themselves known in the most horrendous and cruel fashions.

Posted 07/15/2017

SUMMATION.   Mental health is a very important issue and will be a problem in the future that will have to be dealt with by society. There are very few health facilities that specialize in mental healthcare and only people who are very rich or have insurance that covers mental problems can afford to use those facilities. Many doctors and patients want to address mental health problems with prescription drugs and for many people, this brings stability to their lives and helps them function day to day. However, for other people the prescription drugs cause another problem, addiction, and now the patient is in a more adverse condition because their original problem was never properly diagnosed.

There are many health issues on the verge of affecting the lives of many people. Senior citizens may be facing forms of dementia as they age; athletes who participate in contact sports and soldiers who survived bomb attacks could show symptoms of CTE; people who abuse synthetic drugs, opioids, and painkillers could see their mental capabilities diminish. Stress will continue to be a major problem in society causing many people to suffer mental breakdowns. Attention has to be placed on the mind just as it has been placed on the body to lose weight and stay in shape. Mental disabilities have to be determined at a young age so the person can be treated and learn how to manage their life so they can function in the world.

The Wrong Selection
From The Election
(Beguiled By Campaign Promises)

Donald Trump ran a campaign using vile language and performed despicable acts that angered and appalled many Americans who were embarrassed in front of the world to have a candidate of disgusting character vying to become President. However, there was a large segment of America's population who heard him say he would *"save their jobs," "protect America's borders,"* and *"Make America Great Again!"* and overlooked his crass talk and lewd behavior and voted for him to be the President of the United States. At the onset, it was believed that his supporters were rural and low-income White people but there were people of different races, class, and aspects of life who chose to vote for Trump because he said he would put the issues of Americans first.

It was surprising to many that some people of Muslim faith supported Trump who did not separate them from the terrorists who claimed Islam as their faith as well as people who were Hispanic despite Trump saying he would deport all illegal immigrants and there would not be any extenuating circumstances. President Trump issued a travel ban that made it difficult to return to the U.S. from Muslim countries. Some people were detained for days despite being American citizens and others were not allowed to enter the country. Deportation was initiated against some people who had lived in America but were not citizens. Families were torn apart as fathers, mothers, or children were apprehended to be deported. This included people who were business owners and people who had lived exemplary lives and had not committed any crimes.

A very disturbing revelation was that there were some Black people who supported and voted for Trump. This was despite Trump's documented history of discrimination against Black people and delving into the punishment for imprisoned Black teens. A lawsuit was filed against Trump for not renting apartments in his building to Black people. The settlement of the suit required for Trump to advertise and rent to minorities. In the case of the Central Park jogger who was raped and so severely beaten she could not remember the attack. Five Black and Latino teens were convicted of the crimes and Trump took out a full page ad in a New York newspaper crusading to bring back the death penalty so it could be used to execute the teens. Later, the Central Park 5 would found to be innocent of the crimes and compensated by the state of New York for their time spent in prison. Trump never apologized to the men for the death penalty advertisement and commented that the compensation the men received was too much.

It is regrettable that Americans were so disappointed with the status quo that they elected a self-serving Trump as President. All Americans should be alarmed and aware, especially Black people who could find themselves in a new version of an old institution. A candidate in the future could give speeches like Barack Obama; have the diplomacy of Bill Clinton; be adored like Ronald Reagan; display a down-home demeanor like Jimmy Carter; mystify Americans with stature and charm like John F. Kennedy; yet have the belief and mentality of President Trump. The candidate could appeal to Black people by promising to wipe out unemployment by giving them all jobs, free housing, and security for their children. This candidate will win the Black vote.

All of the promises sound too good to be true and they are, as it is a new form of slavery. There will be jobs but the candidate never mentioned wages or pay; housing is free but the housing will be less than adequate; children will be safe from the police as long as they stay on the property unless they are selected to be sold. It sounds implausible but it is easy to be beguiled by campaign promises when you are the one in need, worried about the future, and not well informed about politics. Americans of all races, religions, and classes must do their due diligence in learning about candidates and informing others so weak candidates can be weeded out and the choice for President will be made from the best candidates because it is presently noticeable that it is easy to make the wrong selection from the election.

Posted 08/12/2017

SUMMATION. During election years, voters listened to candidates makes promises that will be difficult for them to fulfill. They add a catchy slogan to their speeches to drum up interests and gain momentum in the race. More promises will be made to draw in voters who will give their support to the candidate. After years of seeing candidates fail to keep their campaign promises, voters do not really believe their candidate will do everything they have said in their speeches once they win the election. Most voters selected a candidate by how beneficial it will be for them while this person is in office. It is only those who believed the campaign promises that feel they have been fooled and left disappointed.

There were millions of Americans who voted for Donald Trump and millions more who voted for Hillary

Clinton. However, there still were millions who stayed away from the polls and did not cast a vote because they saw no benefit for them with either candidate being in Office. These non-voters are blamed for allowing Trump to win the election but this is by people who would reap benefits from Clinton becoming President. Voters are beginning to see the lies told not only by the candidates but also by the Democratic Party and Republican Party are to distract the people because they are more concerned with representing themselves instead of the people they were elected to represent. Change, however, will be slow because most voters are comfortable with these candidates in spite of their lies rather than choosing the truth and dealing with uncertainty.

No Longer On Her Pedestal
(The White Woman)

She has been presented to the world as the image of beauty; the jewel of the Nile. So stunning that she stirred the oceans, made the wind blow, and settled the sun so it would be more friendlier on a blistering day. Her beauty drove men to write poetry about their unrelenting attraction to her and had them creating songs for their desire to make her their possession. As a young girl she was a princess that brought joy to the world; as a woman she became a queen with moral character and stern structure that helped her rule the world. All this was under the guise of the White man who placed her on a pedestal because she was to be a model of a pristine and perfect woman that he would protect and forbid from any other man.

The White woman accepted this role of being only beneath the White man while being placed above all others and the elite woman of the world. She became entitled and believed those beneath her should step aside and bow at her arrival and serve at her request to be in her presence. By batting her eyes, she could make men give her their fortunes but her words were more powerful as she could cause the deaths of men just by crying out truthfully or dishonestly if she felt she was being disrespected or had been desecrated. Historians and Hollywood producers made her the model for the quintessential woman and the subject of desire in movies for men and beasts and to be admired or envied by other women. She was the standard for beauty and any other woman was beneath her and never placed on a pedestal to be on display to the world.

It was all a facade to establish colonization and set up the White power structure. The White woman was used to help preserve their race by the White man who never gave her true love and respect. Although he kept her on a pedestal, Black men were granted the right to vote before White women by the 14th Amendment. White women were led to believe they were only beneath the White man but had been pushed down politically beneath Black men who were once slaves or descendants of slaves and now had a right denied the prestigious White woman. While on this pedestal, they were sexually starved from the lack of attention they received from the White man who was having sex with women of other ethnic groups, having sex with other men, or having sex with children, preferably little boys.

Once heavily guarded and described as the beauty of the world, the White woman struck a cord of independence by demanding and earning the right to vote, smoking cigarettes in public like a man, and marrying and dating non-White men. Though the White woman was still protected by some White men, other White men allowed her to be exploited by being shown on film having sex with men of different races and also performing sex acts with animals. Pictures were distributed privately among White men and soon there were magazines being published for their viewing pleasure however, the interested and the curious had their senses heightened with the performance of live shows in adult clubs that were legal under the law. The woman of moral character and stern structure was now on exhibit doing lewd and indecent acts for anyone who wanted to see.

During the Civil Rights Movement, some White women chose to demand equal rights for women. They protested by burning their bras in the streets to achieve the right to work on the same job as a man. This burned the bridge between the White man and White woman as she was no longer on the pedestal and openly started dating other women. She was used only as a symbol for the White power structure and her honor was defended but the care and concern for her is gone. Today, she willfully posts her nakedness over social media for attention, she is used to lure Black athletes to play sports at universities, and the birth rate of Whites is so low that White men and White women are marrying people of other ethnic groups in attempts to preserve their race. A distorted history has become a disturbing future for Whites as the truth will correct historians and show the fallacy in the movies of Hollywood producers.

Posted 08/16/2017

SUMMATION. The image and character of the White woman has been presented as the perfect model for the ideal woman. While the ruthlessness of the White man was known, the indiscretions of the White woman were protected to uphold the honorable standard for the chosen woman for female beauty and moral aptitude. However, an in-depth look shows that the White woman was as treacherous as her White man. This was in spite of being treated as less than by her male counterpart because it was more important to maintain being the dominant race and making sure all other groups knew it and accepted it. They endured the brutality delved out to them and groups they labeled inferior by their man in order to remain free of those they considered savages.

It is the White master who is shown as the one

separating Black families by selling members in slavery but in many instances it was at the insistence of the White woman because her husband had fathered a child with a Black slave. The White woman enticed Black women to join their feminist movement but their marriages did not suffer from rules as did the Black woman who could not live with her husband in public housing. Today, the White woman is showing her true character by making 911 calls on law-abiding Black people in hopes of having them arrested or possibly killed by the police for being in places they feel are only for Whites. Now, she has to fight for relevance because of her low birth rate and the rise of ethnic women holding public office in government and executive positions in the business world.

The White Man In The Chimney
(The Charade Is Over)

An awareness is being experienced by many Blacks that is shining a light on the hypocrisy America has portrayed to Blacks to get them to believe they were as American as apple pie. However, this new enlightenment has made Blacks see they are still not considered and not being treated like citizens of the United States which granted Blacks citizenship by order of the 14th Amendment. New laws and political correctness have become a cover for those who despise Blacks to hide their true feelings under and despite the contributions Blacks have made and continue to make in the building of America into a super power, there is a segment of the population who do not consider Blacks Americans and would be happy for them to leave the country.

There were many Blacks who bought in to being part of America, one nation under God, indivisible and justice for all, and *"we are all the same."* Time and time again, Blacks have been shown different after displaying their heroism in wars for the country, performing at high standards that led America to victory against other countries in sporting events, executing mathematical science that helped America advance its space program, and the genius of George Washington Carver whose inventions and discoveries contributed to many industries and helped bolster the American economy. Great accomplishments but it is just as dangerous for a young Black man to go to the neighborhood convenience store and try to return home safely as a soldier trying to cross a field of land mines.

It is time for Blacks to pledge allegiance to a nation of their own instead of to a flag that was raised and country that celebrated independence while their ancestors were enslaved. Although there are many Blacks who believe in a government that considered them property instead of humans at its inception and allowed their land, property, and businesses to be taken (which prevented them from building generational wealth) and never compensated the owners, the charade is over. There is no Santa Claus delivering gifts on Christmas, a bunny rabbit that lays chocolate and candy marshmallow eggs for Easter, and a fairy that leaves money under a pillow for a pulled tooth nor will Blacks ever be fully accepted in America including those who are given fame and celebrity for being entertaining and profitable. This is comparable to Abraham Lincoln giving Black slaves freedom but refusing to grant them equal rights and the same status as Whites.

Chickens and eagles are birds but they not the same. Lynx and tigers are cats but not the same. Geckos and crocodiles are lizards but not the same. Blacks and Whites are people but are not the same. This could be the problem in America and around the world. Uniformity, conventionalism, and synchronicity works well in the military, sports teams, and musical bands but they cannot replace cultural behavior that is learned and passed on generationally. Some animals have the ability to know feeding areas, breeding grounds, migratory routes, and where to go to die from instincts inherited from a member of their species they may have never known. Blacks have similarities with Blacks in Africa, Jamaica, Cuba, and Haiti without ever going to the continent or the Caribbean. Whites have similarities with people in Europe, Russia, Switzerland,

and Australia without visiting these places. Differences of people should be learned, embraced, and respected not forced to be abandon as in the cases of Blacks and Native-Americans.

Tomorrow for Blacks is a new day and they must leave behind bad practices that should not be passed on to future generations. They cannot continue to try to live the American way, they have to live the natural way. All of the habits that are destructive to the Black family and Black community have to end before they both can flourish by establishing themselves culturally instead of nationally. It is imperative that they learn health habits beneficial for them and medicines and medical procedures that are appropriate for their bodies. There is a difference between Blacks and Whites and Blacks should not receive medical treatment meant for Whites and vice versa. Blacks have to teach Blacks education until adulthood. A bear never leaves her cubs with a lion to learn how to survive as a bear. This structure will be difficult and shunned by many but it is time for Blacks to realize there is no White man in the chimney bearing gifts and no matter how hard you try and whatever you accomplish, you will always be seen as Black in America so you may as well be yourself.

Posted 08/17/2017

SUMMATION. As more and more Blacks raise their level of understanding and are able to refute most of what they have been taught in schools and unsubstantiated family traditions, they are being shown how many non-Blacks feel about them and consider them a threat. Knowledge was taken and withheld from Blacks during colonization and slavery to make it easier for them to be controlled and given instruction that would always make them inferior to non-Blacks. It also made Blacks dependent on non-Blacks, this helped their oppressors to become wealthy and powerful while Blacks looked at them as models of success. Black people were lost and trying to find themselves through White images.

The reality for Black people is no matter how they act in compliance, believe in White ideology, and become extremely successful they will always be viewed as Black people. True independence can only come by Blacks knowing who they are and not being told what they are and not trying to live up to White people's idea of who they should be. After slavery ended, some Black leaders wanted Black people to assimilate into American culture but Black people were not welcomed and did not receive equal rights. Future Black generations should remain separate and live among themselves because non-Blacks are making it apparent that no matter how much they copy Black culture they do not want to be associated with Black people.

A Return To Normalcy
(After Charlottesville)

The rally in Charlottesville appalled people around the world. A demonstration in protest of the removal of the Confederate statue Robert E. Lee consisted of White supremacist groups the KKK, neo-Nazi groups, White Nationalists, and Alt-right members who were granted a permit by the city to march. They flooded the street carrying the American flag, the Confederate flag, and swastikas while spewing hateful chants to claim superiority and denigrate other groups of people they oppose. People who disagreed with the bigoted groups, included the protest movement Antifa, confronted them on the street and violence ensued as people were beaten and a woman lost her life when a White supremacist, rammed a car into a crowd of people injured many caught in the path.

President Donald Trump has been ridiculed and lambasted for not convincingly condemning the White supremacist groups and is accused of not being critical of the racist organizations who have openly stated they support the President. The call for impeachment of President Trump has been prevalent since he has taken office and it has increased because of his spiritless response to the hateful protest that many Americans believe is further dividing the country. Some republicans are in agreement with the impeachment of President Trump which would elevate Vice President Mike Pence to Commander In Chief. This is because Trump is an outsider to the establishment and the government's conventional ways which is why a segment of the American population elected him President. Pence has had a career in politics and is ingrained in the establishment with views that are probably worse than Trump's but he follows the order of the government. Trump may be a snake but he has a rattle that makes you aware of him at all times. Pence may also be a snake but he remains hidden and moves about silently giving the impression that he nonthreatening and nonpoisonous but is actually more deadlier than Trump.

Some Black people have been outspoken and motivated to defiant actions since the violent protest and solemn response from President Trump. They have been on the forefront of removing Confederate statues and monuments and instigating the removal of all symbols honoring the Confederacy that is on public property and receiving money from taxpayers to be maintained. An impeachment of President Trump and the removal of some or most of his Cabinet would be a great accomplishment to many Black people because of their racist views but these ideologies and behaviors are not just at the top of government, it is throughout government. White supremacist groups shed their costumes and uniforms long ago and have been dressing in a professional manner for years to infiltrate government and corporate offices.

A misconception is being made by Black people that some part of the rally in Charlottesville was about the issues and welfare of Black people. The people who were protesting and those who were anti-protesting were predominantly White. This was not about a Confederate statue for the anti-protesters. Generations of White people have been raised on rap music, many of them are not just part of an American society, they are members of a global society, and many of them are dating and will marry someone who is non-White and have or will have mixed-race children. They have no connection to the Confederacy and know they are becoming a minority in the United States and are outnumbered by people of color in the rest of the world and they do not want their future to be horrendous like their ancestors made it for people of color.

There is a belief by some Black people that White people are starting to understand their plight and will fight with Black people to make change. However, there have been atrocities and murders of Black people and never have large groups of White people come out in protest for their support. Sean Bell was slaughtered on the eve of his wedding day, Sandra Bland was found dead in jail under police custody, 12-year-old Tamir Rice was killed by police within seconds after their arrival, John Crawford was shot dead by police in Walmart, residents in Flint, Michigan used water contaminated with lead that was approved by government officials but not once did large predominantly White groups take to the streets in protest or speak out defiantly against the system in which they benefit.

A White woman, Justine Diamond, was killed by a policeman of Somalian heritage in Minnesota and no large groups of White people shut down the city in protest for her, either. This is because those who are truly *protected and served* by the police consider this an accidental casualty in the preservation of their way of life and the ability to have peace of mind. After Charlottesville, there is this sentiment to bring Americans together, denounce those in opposition, and speak about a brighter future for America which encourages some Americans however, police will continue to kill Black people which is not making change or the bright future Black people envisioned, it is a return to normalcy.

Posted 08/18/2017

SUMMATION.   America is being held together by the loose thread of *Old Glory.* Americans have chosen their sides and dug in firmly as President Donald Trump shows no signs of trying to bring the country together. A White woman was killed at the march in Charlottesville and President Trump reluctantly gave her acknowledgment. Heather Heyer was in opposition of those marching to not have Confederate monuments removed and almost ignored by Trump who never condemned the marchers. The President caused more division by making a derogatory remark toward NFL players who were protesting during the playing of the National Anthem. He said the players were disrespecting the Anthem, the Flag, and military veterans but never addressed the reason for the protests, police brutality and the unarmed shooting of Black people.

As the complexion of America changes, those who believe in the old ways are intent on preserving them and their heritage. They support the President's crackdown on illegal immigration and the deportation of children who have known America as their only home. In contrast, there is a segment of the population who want Trump impeached for his alleged involvement with Russia who many believed interfered with the 2016 Presidential Election. This has deeply fractured the nation and given rise to such groups as those who marched in Charlottesville. It will not be a surprise to see a grand march in Washington, D.C. as staged by the KKK in 1920.

Attorneys for the police officer who shot and killed Justine Diamond are trying to get the criminal case dismissed by the judge. The attorneys maintain that Mohamed Noor acted reasonably but prosecutors state Noor was reckless in using deadly force causing the death of Diamond charging him with murder and manslaughter. A $50 million civil rights lawsuit has been filed by John Ruszczyk, the father of Diamond, accusing Noor, city officials, and law enforcement of conspiring to cover up facts involved with the shooting and intentionally leaving the body cameras off after the incident. A hearing ended without a ruling by U. S. Magistrate Judge Tony Leung on whether to delay the civil trial.

Profits Made From
The Courageous
(The Business of War)

On September 20, 2001, President George Bush declared war on Afghanistan to fight against the Taliban and Al Qeada. Many Americans approved and supported the President's decision because they believed it was in response to the terrorist attacks in New York City and Washington, D.C. Two Presidents and 16 years later, there are American troops still in Afghanistan and President Donald Trump and his administration is trying to find a reason to send more troops to continue the war. Most of those patriotic Americans who were enthusiastic about going to war to avenge the attack on their country are now visibly silent about the war or outraged that American troops are still their fighting.

America went through a great recession that caused many Americans to lose most of their savings, homes, and jobs. This while the American government was spending millions of dollars a day on a war that its citizens no longer wanted to continue and bailing out financial institutions who suffered astronomical losses from mismanagement. President Barack Obama was elected on the belief he would end the war and bring American troops home. Although the President did bring some troops back to the United States, the war continued which caused many American families to experience the loss of a child, father, mother, husband, or wife from being killed in battle or having to be a caretaker to a soldier who has returned with life-long wounds and injuries or post-traumatic stress disorder (PTSD).

Afghanistan is a country that has been involved in wars where the British and Soviet Union retreated because it was too difficult to win battles in the terrain. There were some war strategists who believed America would endure the same fate and after 16 years, many Americans are realizing this is not about winning a war and stamping out radical Islamic terrorists. Americans were led into war by the business interest of those who profit from wars and who wanted to profit from the 1 trillion dollar mineral deposits and oil reserves in Afghanistan. A war that was started and continues is only benefiting those who started it and has no chance of losing their life while many will be casualties of this war and soldiers will return home to have to fight for their benefits and medical treatment they have earned and deserve that is a small percentage of what those in business have earned in Afghanistan from the service of the soldiers.

An opioid epidemic has affected many American families through drug addiction, death, or both. Heroin addiction is so prevalent in America that an antidote is being used to revive those who have suffered an overdose. Some people who support the war in Afghanistan have not connected the uptick in opioid use in America and the poppy fields in Afghanistan which were being protected by American soldiers to prevent from being destroyed during the war. A multi-billion dollar industry that is kept secret by those who profit in the trade of opioids which is another way those in business are allowing people to die while they make a profit.

War is being used as a business and industry under the guise of patriotism and loyalty to country. A strategical plan by those in power is used on citizens to encourage them to volunteer to fight for those who propose war but do not face the consequence of death or injury. If those who insist on war would have to go into the Coliseum and fight for survival like the gladiators, engage in a duel to live or die, or go on the battlefield and experience the sights, sounds, and smells of death, they may not have the propensity to declare war. Until those who volunteer and support war make sure there is a necessity for war, there will continue to be those who profit from their courage while those who serve are maimed, killed, and mentally affected and their families bear loss, hardship, and life-long debilitation.

Posted 08/22/2017

SUMMATION. The opioid epidemic has devastated White America with addiction, poor health, and death. The U.S. Government is approaching it differently than it did the crack epidemic that primarily wreaked havoc in Black communities. Instead of enacting laws as it was done to Black people to stop the use of crack cocaine, medical attention and health care is being provided to White drug users. They are not being incarcerated for long sentences causing their families to be separated but it is having a disruptive effect on White families as they are suffering a low birth rate and many Whites are in mixed relationships because of this drug addition running rampantly within their race.

Still, many people have not connected it with the military presence of the U.S. in Afghanistan. Life is sacrificed for profit. This has been a pattern for the U.S. as it learned while it was suffering through the Great Depression. The U.S. was still struggling economically ten years after the crash of the stock market in 1929 and the country was the midst of another economic downfall. In 1941, the U.S. entered World War II sending many unemployed men to battle or working for manufacturing companies to build military equipment and supplies for the war. Businesses employed women due to the shortage of men who had become servicemen. After the war ended in 1945, the economy would dip the next four years as peacetime production was not as profitable as during the war. The U.S. would enter the Korean War in 1950. War is being disguised as a necessary act in defense of a country but in actuality, war is an industry that provides revenue for those who never have to enter battle.

Commitment and
Support For Equality
(A United Front Is Needed In The NFL)

There was an assumption made by many people that the protests of the National Anthem in the NFL would cease without Colin Kaepernick playing in the league however, players across the league have been taking a knee, raising a fist, or in a posture of non-observance during the performance of the Star-Spangled Banner. This is detestable to NFL owners, many coaches, players, and fans who feel social activism has no place in sports although, many of the players in the NFL are Black and a portion came from impoverished and heavily policed communities that Kaepernick wanted to expose to force change in laws and the behavior of law enforcement.

Some Blacks felt the protests would be more profound with the participation of White players and a segment of them answered the call and joined in the protests. Still, the reason Kaepernick started protesting is being overlooked as many in the media are wanting him to come out and speak about the issues of his protest and to find out if he truly wants to play football or is his activism more important than the game. However, those in the media are not questioning politicians and lawmakers in local, state, and federal governments about police brutality and inequality experienced by Blacks nor are they queried about police reform, reviewing police requirements, and punishment for police who unlawfully kill unarmed Blacks. The directive is to ridicule Kaepernick to keep the focus off of his reasons for protesting.

While White players are volunteering themselves

into the protests, current and former Black NFL players are laying blame at the feet of Kaepernick who has not been signed by an NFL team and it appears he will not play in the league this season. Some of these Black men proclaim to be doing work in Black communities but at a time when NFL players are trying to form solidarity in the league, these Black individuals want the issue to be about Kaepernick playing football instead of the issues of his protest. There are Black players who refused to protest in fear of suffering a financial loss and others who pledge allegiance to the Flag and National Anthem and choose to speak out against the protests which stunts the growth of a formidable unification among the players. A power that most do not realize is in their possession.

In 1965, the American Football League held its All-Star game in New Orleans which was continuing the system of segregation and ignoring the 1964 Civil Rights Act that was signed to end it. Black AFL players had to deal with racism after arriving at the airport as White cab drivers refused them service and they were not allowed in hotels, restaurants, and clubs downtown. A restaurant owner refused to serve Black AFL player Ernie Ladd and then pulled out his gun to force him on his way. Abner Haynes (a star player in the league) and Cookie Gilchrist (the AFL's best player) led a boycott of the game and had the approval of the other 19 Black players who were to play in the game. The AFL had a large number of Black players from Black colleges and the players new they had power and enforced it.

White players found out about the boycott and did not want to play the game without the Black players. Ron Mix, Jack Kemp, and other White players supported the boycott by the Black players and helped form a powerful group of solidarity that forced AFL commissioner Joe Foss to move the game to Houston.

Haynes and Gilchrist faced retribution from the AFL as they were traded by the Kansas City Chiefs and Buffalo Bills soon after the All-Star game. Their salaries were paltry when compared with the earnings of the players of today but their dignity and respect were more important to them and this motivated them to stand on their principals. The AFL would merge with the NFL in 1966 and New Orleans would be granted a franchise in 1967 after it ended the discrimination policies of local businesses.

Many Black players are bound to the NFL with fame and fortune just as Black slaves were bound to the plantation with chains and fear. In both systems, some are content with their environment and dare not do anything to upset it. A great number of players keep their heads down and fight for an extra yard for their team but they fail to realize a united front is needed in the NFL so the players can form a resilient unit to fight together. They are the product that drives a multi-billion dollar business but they are made to keep their helmets on so they can only be seen as a team and not as a person and are only allowed to speak when asked a question. White players saw the racial hatred at the rally and protest in Charlottesville and have decided to make a commitment and support Black players in their fight for equality but this is the Black players' fight and they must stand up, unify, and lead because if they continue to squabble with each other and not make use of their power they will continue to be a source of income for others and cause future generations to be weak.

Poster 08/31/2017

SUMMATION.   The protests of Colin Kaepernick is

still an irritant to the NFL even though he is not playing quarterback for a team. Other players have taken a knee or protested in their own manner to the dislike of NFL management. Players have learned their work relationship in the league is not employer and employee but actually owner and property. NFL owners want their players to perform on the field, keep their heads in the game, and leave all issues outside of the game off the field. An upstanding image of the league is what the owners want presented to the fans without any shade being thrown on *"The Shield."*

It is being shown to the players that the owners are too concerned with their bottom lines and the fans with their fantasy sports to give any attention to police brutality and the killing of unarmed Black people by police. Many of these players who they want to just play are from overpoliced communities and it would seem owners and fans would be interested in preventing the murders of possible NFL stars of the future. However, they are more concerned with the disrespect of the National Anthem, the Flag, and military veterans (which is not the case) instead of appealing to Kaepernick's suggestion of being more stringent on selecting police officers and have a very intensive training course and a longer period of instruction for applicants to be qualified as officers. As long as the owners and most fans are safe in their neighborhoods, they can care less about what happens in Black communities.

Patriotism Used As A Weapon
(Trump Reviles Black Athletes)

The speech by President Donald Trump in Alabama has shown that the American fabric is frayed and the thread that holds it together is worn. In his speech, he used crass words to ridicule athletes who protest during the National Anthem which drew applause and support from most of the people in attendance. Black athletes are leading the majority of the protests in order to gain attention and force change for Black people who are dealing with inequality, injustice, and police brutality and shootings. White people led the cheers during the President's speech because they feel the Flag and the National Anthem are being disrespected and these athletes could not earn their million dollar salaries without the rights the Flag represents and the sacrifice of veterans.

Those in support of the POTUS believe the athletes are being unpatriotic and are disrupting their time with their family and friends to enjoy sporting events. These are the same people who do not bat an eye or raise their voice after seeing an unarmed Black person gunned down by the police on a video and the officer later acquitted in court or found to have acted appropriately. However, they stand with a person who never entered military service and avoided being drafted six times but still has the audacity to demean Senator John McCain who is a veteran of the Vietnam War and had to endure the atrocities of being captured but refused to be released until other soldiers had been allowed to leave. Yet, no one has called the President and his supporters as being unpatriotic.

There are many who believe President Trump is

targeting Black athletes for protesting and not being grateful for their million dollar contracts, fame, and the ability to live a comfortable life with racist rhetoric that inflames White supremacists and stretches the thread that holds America together. It gives those that hate the protests the belief that the Black athletes are not employed by their employers but are owned by their owners and that they should enjoy and take advantage of their popularity and embrace the good life afforded them from playing sports. However, some Black athletes cannot sit idly by and watch Black people suffer unjustly and become victims of unwarranted killings by the police.

Although the POTUS condemned the protest, the Black athlete nay not have been his aim. Their is a belief that this is an attempt at retaliation by President Trump against the NFL to make them suffer the loss of viewership and revenue for not allowing him to have a team in the league after he lost his team when the USFL dissolved. Another target could be television networks for their critical commentaries of him during his Presidential campaign and NBC for their abrupt separation with him on the show *The Apprentice* in order to cause the networks a loss of profits. There were 7 NFL owners who donated and supported the campaign of Trump which could be his strategy to penetrate his true target so he can draw support to put pressure on Republicans to repeal Obamacare.

It will be a phenomenal failure for President Trump and his administration if Obamacare is not repealed and replaced with their own Affordable Care Act. Senator McCain has prevented the repeal from passing and more Republicans are following his lead. Many see the speech in Alabama by the President as an effort to draw support from his base but his target was rich White Republicans who can help him get Obamacare repealed by persuading Republican Senators to vote for it. The protesters in Charlottesville and the supporters at the Alabama speech can only cheer after hearing the hateful and derogatory comments but they cannot pass legislation.

President Trump may have reviled Black athletes but it was only a means to an end as he is not concerned with those who get paid but with those who can pay people. The actions are being presented as racist and tasteless by the President and disrespectful and unpatriotic by Black athletes but this was a chess move for a greater reward than getting Black athletes to honor the Flag. Patriotism was used as a weapon by the POTUS to incite the masses of *"patriots"* who honor the Flag and the National Anthem for 3-4 minutes a week but talk and debate all week about Black players on their fantasy teams. These same *"patriots"* then watch the football games on Sunday after the Black players have showed their patriotism by protesting the injustice of their people before the game.

Posted 09/26/2017

SUMMATION. The inflammatory remarks by President Donald Trump about Black NFL players protesting during the playing of the National Anthem resounded loudly throughout the athletic world. This opened the eyes of many Black athletes who believed America and the world had finally learned to accept Black people for who they are and their contributions to society but in actuality they are treated as a commodity just as the Black people who were held in bondage during slavery. It is hard for many to comprehend this reality when some Black players have multi-million dollar contracts paid to them by their million dollar owners who earn profits from their play. During slavery, there were Black slaves who were paid services and their owners profited from this working arrangement.

There are former and present Black players who disagree with the protests of the Black players because they have prospered from the opportunities afforded them because of playing in the NFL. They are successful because they followed the rules and earned their money but they neglect to think of those who were harassed and killed by the police in their communities and the possibilities of it happening to their children. While they speak fondly and are appreciative of their team owner for helping them become financially comfortable, there are many former NFL players who are suffering and need health care but are being ignored by the NFL and team owners. The Black players who are protesting are facing the same problem as Black slaves who wanted their freedom. Those who look like them, those who they know, those who they care about have an affinity to the owners and are comfortable with their positions and would rather hope for change than to cause change.

Senator John McCain died on August 25, 2018 but the animosity between he and President Trump continued as the Senator did not want the President at his funeral but did want Vice President Mike Pence in attendance. Trump gave a somber condolences to McCain's family and said he would not attend the funeral to prevent causing security problems for the family and their guests.

A Slow Death For Gladiators
(NFL Players and CTE)

An examination of Aaron Hernandez brain showed signs of a severe case of CTE (chronic trauma encephalopathy) that is usually found in the brain of a 67 year-old person. This is significant because Hernandez was only 27 years-old when he committed suicide in a jail cell. The examination showed Hernandez suffered from an advanced stage 3 CTE which can be caused by repeated head trauma that may occur in contact sports. It has been synonymous with NFL players due to many ex-players dying with their brain showing damage from head trauma and significant signs of CTE and some former players developing symptoms of the brain affliction. There is a reluctance by former football players to give importance to the examination because of Hernandez's criminal past and that he made the choice to play football but they cannot deny that the CTE Hernandez suffered from is as real as the death suffered by his victim.

A vast number of football players come from impoverished backgrounds and challenging economic conditions who saw playing pro football as a way to improve their life and help their families. Many former players are so appreciative of their opportunity to play in the NFL and the financial gains they earned during their careers that they are reluctant to speak out against the NFL and the effects of CTE. Despite the possibility that many of them may develop symptoms of CTE, they do not regret playing football and would do it all over again. The revelations about CTE have not deterred former players from inspiring young boys to play but the concern of parents has caused a decrease in participation in youth football which has made some youth leagues cancel their football season.

Football players are comparable with the gladiators who fought at the Colosseum in Rome because they play in magnificent stadiums before ruckus crowds who wants their team to pulverize the other team. Fans cheer at hard-hit collisions just as people roared in the Colosseum when gladiators collided. Applause is afforded a player taken off the field on his back just as applause ranged out when the lifeless body of a gladiator was removed from the Colosseum. Some football players want their sons to follow their path into football in spite of the injuries and their long-term effects they may experience. It is hard to see a gladiator wanting his son to follow in his footsteps when the son would ultimately be facing death each time he entered the Coliseum. A sense of invincibility may be blurring the sensibility of former football players who know the possibility of injury but refuse to accept the inevitability of CTE.

Many adults who have taken life chances to attain success want their children to take a less dangerous road to prosperity. They know the luck and the breaks they got may not occur for their children so they work hard to give their children the opportunities they did not receive. Ex-NFL players are able to help their children and other youth get opportunities that were not accessible to them at that age by many teaching the youth the game of football and the correct way to play it while speaking colorfully about the riches and fame of playing in the NFL but seldom about the injuries and long-term pain. The connection between NFL players and CTE is real no matter who is denying it and the time has come for it to be accepted. For many gladiators of the gridiron, it has been a slow and agonizing death but in the future, death may come much sooner. Once again, Aaron Hernandez was only 27 years-old.

Posted 09/27/2017

SUMMATION.   Football is still one of America's favorite sports and there are many young players who are dreaming of playing in the NFL one day. However, some of the luster has been removed from *"The Shield"* that is widely known across the country. Some fans who opposed or supported the protests by Black NFL players stopped watching the game in past seasons but many of those fans could no longer miss seeing their favorite players and teams play. A much bigger problem for the NFL is parents who will not let their sons play the game anymore for fear of long term injuries with brain trauma being the most important. There has been a major lack of participation in some youth leagues that caused their season to be canceled.

A trend with younger players in the NFL is to retire before the age of 30 to lessen the chance of suffering from CTE. The severity of concussions have become known to players and they see the problems former players are having from brain trauma with some ending in an early death. Some athletes are hanging up their football cleats in college as they are aware of the problems that can occur from multiple concussions. There are new rules in the NFL put in place to prevent helmet to helmet contact as the league tries to get players to avoid using their helmets in collisions. It is going to take some time for players to learn to play in this manner just as it is taking time to learn the effects on the brain from years of concussions.

126

Breaking Through The Ice
(Leave Cardi B Alone)

At a time when President Donald Trump has made asperse remarks about Black players protesting the inequality, injustices, and police brutality experienced by Black people during the National Anthem of NFL games, made comments in a delayed response that contemned Puerto Rico after the island and its people were devastated by Hurricane Maria, and is trying to repeal Obamacare, Cardi B has the No. 1 song on the Billboard Hot 100 chart. *"Bodak Yellow"* became the first song to hold the top spot by a female solo rapper in 19 years when Lauryn Hill reigned with her No. 1 hit, *"Doo Wop (That Thing)."*

The contrast between the two female rappers is very distinctive as Hill spit pro-Black, positive, and empowering lyrics to Cardi B's ratchet, vulgar, and street rhymes that are pervasive in rap music. Cardi B's rise to the top is being seen as a method to distract people (especially Black people) from the pertinent issues of the day. As Black people are trying to rise together in demand of not only their equal rights but their human rights, some Black people see *"Bodak Yellow"* as a divisive attempt to keep a segment of Black people in a party mode and concerned with material things rather than filling the ranks of protests and speaking out on political and social issues that makes a large portion of Americans uncomfortable.

Cardi B has been outspoken and candid about her occupation and struggles before her musical career. Born Belcalis Almanzar to a Trinidadian mother and Dominican father, she endured poverty, gang life, dropping out of college, and an abusive relationship with a boyfriend. She became an exotic dancer as a means to support herself and it provided her with opportunities to improve her life. By the use of social media, she was able to gain a following on Vine and Instagram and later, she made her appearance on television in the series *Love & Hip Hop: New York* which has led to a great start to a musical career and opportunities to be successful in the fashion industry.

For all of the naysayers and detractors, leave Cardi B alone! At the lowest time of this young lady's life, there were very few who gave her support and lifted her up and now that she has reached heights that many could not imagine for her, stop trying to tear her down. Many Black people give in to the belief of others about them and feel they have limited capabilities when they should belief their capabilities are unlimited. Most Black people know when to be stylish and acquisitive and when to have a good time and party as well as when to exhibit their activism by fighting in the streets, in the media, and in the courtroom for the rights of their people. Do not criticize Cardi B for breaking through the frozen ice of poverty to become a success. She has excelled in a male-dominated industry and will be an inspiration to young girls whether many like it or not. While she has their attention, encourage her to become a leader in her own right and motivate young girls to greatness by placing higher expectations on her to become knowledgeable and supportive of social issues instead of stigmatizing her as another ratcheted, self-indulgent rapper.

Posted 09/29/2017

SUMMATION.   Reaching a high level of success in a short period of time has made life challenging for

Cardi B. After having success with *"Bodak Yellow"*, she released her debut album in April of 2108 and it was certified gold on the first day. In a secret wedding, she married Offset of the Migos in September of 2017 and delivered their first child in July of 2018. Cardi B took time to spend with her newborn instead of going on tour with Bruno Mars. Her fans were waiting for her when she did start touring to see one of their favorite artists perform live in concert. The rap artists never totally went away as she let her fans know what was going on in her life through social media. Maybe sharing too much information for some but Cardi B has never been shy about expressing herself.

As Cardi B reached the top of the music world, she started being compared with Nicki Minaj. Although Cardi B showed Nicki respect for her accomplishments in rap, the feeling did not seem to be mutual. Some fans felt Cardi had replaced Nicki as best female rapper and this appeared to bother the *"Queen of hip hop"* who released a successful album in August of 2018 but it seemed Cardi still had the attention of the rap world. It all came to a head in New York at Harper's Bazaar Icons party when the two women had a verbal altercation that almost became physical with Cardi receiving an accidental blow from a bodyguard that caused swelling on her forehead. This incident was unfortunate and untimely for the two rappers who have the ability to sway the attention on rap music to the female side of the game. After decades of women being only sex objects in music videos, these two women may be missing an opportunity to bring female MC's to the front of rap music.

True Revolutionaries
(Black Women On The Forefront)

A symbol that had flown for decades in honor of those who lost a war and meant to represent segregation in southern states and further repress a people who had been oppressed for generations had to come down. In an historic act that is equal to the patriotic stories told in school, Bree Newsome climbed the flag pole on the state grounds of Columbia, SC to remove the Confederate flag which snowballed into the removal of other Confederate monuments and symbols. A light was beamed on those references to Confederacy that were offensive to Black people and not acceptable to a population that is becoming more diverse. After flying over the state of South Carolina for move than 50 years, the Confederate flag was moved to the state's *"relic room"* by the governor.

While President Donald Trump is allowed to use social media to send out his outlandish tweets, others are being prohibited from offering their intelligent opinions through social networks. Jemele Hill has been unabashedly outspoken about her criticism of the President. She called the POTUS a *"White supremacist"* which made some people call for ESPN (Hill's employer) to fire her but after meeting with executives Hill apologized. Due to the actions of Trump, it was hard to refute her comments. When Jerry Jones forbid any of the Dallas Cowboys from kneeling during the National Anthem, Hill suggested for those who support the protects to contact advertisers to show their disapproval on Jones's stance.

ESPN suspended Hill claiming she violated their social media policy but she has drawn support from Black women's group to have her reinstated.

Stepping out ahead of Black college football players, cheerleaders of Kennesaw State College took a knee during the National Anthem to draw attention to police brutality and other social issues. This is a monumental act by the female students who show they are concerned about the killing of unarmed Black people by the police and are contributing their efforts to bring about change and new policy in law enforcement. However, it will not come as quickly as the new policy inserted by KSU administrators a few days after the cheerleaders protested that will not allow the group to kneel at any more games although the administrators claim the policy was under consideration before the protest by the cheerleaders.

After hearing the derogative comment by Trump about NFL players who are protesting during the National Anthem, Rep. Sheila Jackson Lee took a knee on the floor of the House of Representatives in support of the athletes and in defense of the First Amendment. Although the Star-Spangled Banner was not playing when she knelt, her point was that taking a knee in front of the flag during the National Anthem is not prohibited by the First Amendment. Lee knelt to honor the freedom that gives the President the right to speak rudely about the NFL players which is also the same freedom that gives the athletes the right to protest in a peaceful manner with respect.

Throughout history in the United States, the Black woman has been on the forefront in fighting for the rights of Black people. It was Harriet Tubman who led several Black slaves to freedom without ever being captured. Ida B. Wells begin the anti-lynching campaign and wrote about the lynching of Black people who had not committed any crimes in her newspaper. Sojourner Truth spoke out to end slavery and for human rights and made the phenomenal speech *"Ain't I a Woman?"* in the struggle for women's rights. Black women are true revolutionaries who have lead the way to progress for Black people in many instances. Their contributions to better the lives of Black people are too great to be ignored and are needed in the future to help Black people rise out of the state of oppression.

Posted 10/13/2017

SUMMATION.   Being outspoken has cost Jemele Hill her position at ESPN who bought out her contract so she could be released. The talented Hill has received an opportunity from LeBron James to work on a sports documentary headed by James and his business partner Maverick Carter. Tommia Dean has not been as fortunate as she and all but one of the cheerleaders for Kennesaw State University who protested by taking a knee before football games are no longer on the cheerleading squad. School officials states the reason as there were better participants at the tryouts and they were selected for the squad. Dean is suing the university for violating her civil rights.

Black women are making strides in politics by winning elections in several offices across many states. London Breed became the first Black woman elected mayor of San Francisco. Stacie Abrams is the Democratic Party nominee for governor of Georgia becoming the first Black woman to be a major party nominee for governor in the United States. Diedre DeJear was elected secretary of state in Iowa making her the first Black woman to win a major party nomination for statewide office in the state. Ayanna Pressley won the Democratic Primary in Massachusetts and won the general election to become the first Black woman to represent the state in Congress. Jahana Hayes became the first Black Democrat to serve in Congress for Connecticut when she won the general election. Minnesota state Representative Ilhan Ohan was elected to Congress making her one of the first Muslim women to be members (Rashida Tlaib the other). In Alabama, 36 Black female candidates are running for various offices. Texas saw 19 Black women judges contending for various judicial seats in Houston win their elections. The makeup of the political spectrum is changing and it is being led by Black women.

Finding The Right Time
and The Right Words
(Ending A Relationship)

It has been over for quite some time but you continue to go through the motions of being in a relationship. The time spent in building the relationship and forming ties makes it difficult to bring it to an end. Contemplating whether to stay or to go, that these sour feelings will past and things will get better, or to stick it out when deep down you know its over troubles the mind. However, it is still hard to walk away from someone who is not only your lover but your true friend that you love unconditionally but for some reason it is time to bring it to an end. Whatever attracted you to each other, made you laugh at the same things, and build your own world is now worn and can no longer sustain the relationship.

This is a person who has seen you at your lowest and you have seen them at their lowest and you both consoled and supported each other until things got better for both of you. The experience of the death of a family member showed both of you when you were most vulnerable however, you were that solid rock for each other to stand on to regain your balance so you could move on with your lives. Attraction and desire may have brought you two together but these experiences formed a stronger bond that held you two together. These strong ties are very difficult to break because they cannot be undone. They should not be undone but the past becomes open when the future is torn apart.

There is care and concern but you know they are

going to be hurt and you are going to see the pain in their face when you tell them it is over. Even though they may have similar feelings as you and know there are problems in the relationship, they are not ready for it to end. They want to figure out what is wrong with the relationship and make the changes needed to save it. Being in agreement with each other about the relationship should end is still difficult because it brings about change that they are not ready to deal with and it fills them with trepidation in moving forward. In all circumstances, there will be hurt and pain that will sting both of you for some time no matter how delicate you are with the situation.

Looking for the right time to reveal your true feelings overwhelms your mind. You search for the right words to say that are going to be painful nonetheless, in spite of the sentiment and tone you use in your expression. There are birthdays, holidays, and family gatherings and also invitations to parties by friends that get in the way and make you put off telling of your distressful decision. It is as much a reprieve for you as it is an avoidance of sorrow for your lover but you know it has to be done because you can no longer linger in this relationship. So, it may be a good day for them that you hate to disrupt or it may be one of their worst days that you are reluctant to pile on. However, you are determined and have build up the courage to say, "It's over."

Posted 11/25/2017

SUMMATION.   It happens to couples of all races, all ages, and of any social status. Popularity and riches cannot prevent it nor does faith and fidelity. Couples break up, fall in and out of love more than it is known and maybe people do not want to think about it because it could happen to their relationship. Although in many of these relationships, people know in the beginning that it is not going to last long term. Some people like to have someone to date until they meet the person they find attractive and compatible while others are just dating to keep from being lonely. This is not fair to the other person who may believe they are headed to a permanent situation or ignoring the signs that it is not serious and is only a temporary relationship.

The end for some couples is caused by outside agitation. A couple may be in love or trying to get to know each other because they want their relationship to work but someone outside of the relationship may break up the couple because they desire one of the couple for themselves or they are jealous of the couple's happiness because they do not have anyone. It is hard to determine how relationships are going as a couple that laughs and is always happy can have more problems than a couple that argues and fights consistently. A break up can be so disparaging for some that it can lead to violence. This may happen because one may be more invested than the other in the relationship. There has to be thought and concern given to someone when breaking up with them and still, with this consideration there is never a good time to end a relationship.

A Share Of The Blame
(Black Responsibility)

It is known by most Blacks that systemic oppression and discrimination exits in America. They know that many American citizens have difficult lives but they realize that Blacks have never been accepted as citizens of America. Their lives are made difficult by laws and policies that other citizens benefit from or are oblivious to and by the people who enforce these laws and introduce these policies. Images and stereotypes are presented of Blacks to give negative impressions to other groups of people to show why the unjust laws and discriminatory policies are necessary and must be enforced on people who are portrayed as having a lack of social responsibility.

Many Black people know those in the legal system are out to have them arrested so they can populate prisons or have them put on probation to pay hefty fees and absurd fines when they were not able to hire an attorney. These are known hazards in the lives of many Black people who find them troublesome and unavoidable because they are targets in an unjust society. Knowing their communities are over policed and they often experience being detained without breaking the law, it would seem they would have no intentions of engaging in crimes or be associated with anyone doing illegal activities. However, they not only continue to live in these cities but commit crimes that lead to long prison sentences or are subjected to routine arrests by police that cause them to appear frequently in court.

Blacks who have dysfunction in their families because of drug abuse still choose to use drugs and suffer the same consequences experienced by other family members. This often causes many of them to face drug arrests, time in prison, and medical and health problems that some will blame on the system of oppression but no one is forcing them to use drugs or drink alcohol every month, every week, or every day. It is true that these substances are made easily accessible in Black communities but most Blacks are willful participants and users who contribute to these businesses which help them stay in their communities.

There is an anger among many Black men about the child support system. They feel that it takes advantage of them by taking a substantial percentage of their incomes along with added fees. Those who fall behind accrue interest and sometimes are jailed if they cannot pay what they owe which causes them to accrue more interest and possibly court fees. Some Black men are irresponsible and refuse to pay child support to their children which may cause the mother and child to become dependent on the welfare system and receive food stamps. This dilemma can be avoided by Black men and women if they take measures to prevent having a child or be willing participants and contributors to raising their child without being part of any system.

A Black life in America is often filled with strife but Blacks have to take responsibility for their decisions. Blacks are subjected to the rigors of an oppressive system in America that causes problems for every generation and prevents them from being respected as a group of people and their issues recognized by their government but they must take a share of the blame. Blacks complain about the system and fight the system but some allowed themselves to be controlled by the system from making poor choices. There are a segment of Blacks who believe they can help change the system by becoming part of it but they also become controlled by it from receiving high salaries and social status. The only way to change the system is to weaken it. Better decisions by Blacks to prevent being arrested and avoid court cases and long prison sentences dilutes its effect. A committed plan by Blacks that can be sustain for generations is the way to bring an end to the system of oppression.

Posted 11/29/2017

SUMMATION.   The shooting of Botham Jean by police officer Amber Guyger in Dallas has the attention of many people. Jean was shot in his apartment by Guyger who claims she thought she was in her apartment. Guyger, who is White, is charged with manslaughter but many Blacks want her charged with the murder of Jean, born in St. Lucia, Haiti, who became an American citizen. An investigation is ongoing and Black people are watching as Texas officials try to demean the character of Jean. This is a very important incident that can be listed with the other shootings of unarmed Black men that gained the attention of the world but crimes that are just as heinous are overlooked by Black people and the Black community.

A Black person taking the life of another Black person is not viewed in the same manner as the murder of a Black person at the hands of a White person. Blacks killing each other has become a commonality with no appeal to Black people and entertainment for the rest of the world. However, Black people want dignity and respect shown to Black lives when their own behavior shows they do not care about Black lives. After years of hate and violence experienced by Black people at the hands of non-Blacks, there is no solidarity among Black people to address their problems instead, Blacks have adopted the same mentality that leads to them killing each other. Blacks will have to become a responsible people before they can become a powerful people.

The Rise of The Machines
(Welcome To "Westworld")

Robots have been tasked to do many jobs in this modern world from increasing production in manufacturing, solving intricate economic equations in finance to handling domesticated chores in the home. They have found their place in today's society and one of them have received full citizenship. A robot named Sophia that is constructed with facial recognition, able to process natural language, has advanced artificial intelligence, and is equipped with a synthetic human face has been granted citizenship by Saudi Arabia. Sophia is able to have conversations with humans as she answered questions after giving a brief speech thanking Saudi Arabia for making her the first robot in the world to attain citizenship. The artificial intelligence of the robot is able to evolve as she demonstrated by declaring equal rights for robots that are afforded to humans.

This comes at a time when many people have been displaced from their homes, cities, native lands and countries and are not being welcomed in foreign lands by the citizens and their government. President Donald Trump is trying to remove immigrants who have worked in America for decades because they are illegal. Many of them have had children who have graduated from high school and are working to attain higher education or have achieved a college degree. However, Trump wants to deport these children from their homeland to a country and place they have never known. Some of their parents have already been forced from the country and there is no plan being put in place to help the parents of children gain citizenship.

There have always been those who wanted to cleanse the world of the people who were considered a drag on society, undesirables who were unable to make a solid contribution to the world. They looked different, acted unusual, and were told they were animalistic, inferior by those who claimed to be superior. Robots are made with super intelligence to advance humanity and will have the potential to dilute the population of those without a purpose. In a matter of years, robots are gaining citizenship and seeking equal rights that many groups of humans have been fighting to attain for centuries. And it will all be done under the guise of orders from the robots when it was what those in power wanted all along.

Welcome to *"Westworld"* or any other sci-fi creation where robots were allowed to integrate into society and humans went along with the plan and continued their daily routines unaware they were being overtaken by the artificial humans with a super intelligence. The ability to advance the world and make life better for people is the appeal that causes humans to be susceptible to robots and naive of their capabilities. The rapid improvement of technology draws people to the robots but the humanlike features fascinates many of them and whatever their relationships are deficient of with humans they are rectified with the use of robots.

As robots are being made to use for every facet of life, the affection of sex robots is becoming so common that it is causing a negative effect on the population in some countries. Some may believe this will reduce the participation in *"the world's oldest profession"* and the transference of sexual diseases but it is actually reducing relationships between men and women which is not helping increase the birthrate of the elite. While those in power continue their attempt at controlling the population of those they consider inferior, it is their population that decreases with every decade. They are so focused on maintaining power over the downtrodden that they do not see the rise of the machines as being capable of ending their reign.

Posted 12/19/2017

SUMMATION.   In the past, there was not much use of technology and it was known as *simpler times*. Today, it can be known as *easier times* because technology is used consistently by many people around the world. People can live in isolated areas and still be connected to the rest of the world through technology. For those who want to escape to a new world, there is virtual reality where a person can exist in a lifelike world or they can create one of their own. New technology has been designed to study people to make suggestions based on their habits and are able to control products without instructions from the owners.

Robots are no longer toys played with by children or only seen in the movies possibly played by a human. They are in the real world being used by people everyday and have become part of humans of have suffered a loss of a body part. As technology brought people from all over the world together, it has also caused less interaction between people in real life. People can be seen using some device while having dinner at restaurant and not talking to other people at the table. It is easier for people to interact with technology that is programmed than to deal with the inadequacies and inconsistency of people. Sex robots, a personal voice assistant in the car, robots to do chores in the home, and virtual reality is here and will expand in the future. A conversation between two real people will become rare as handwriting, letters, and postcards.

Losing Faith In A Sunday Ritual
(NBA Supplants The NFL)

As the NFL struggles to complete a tempestuous season, it has lost many followers along the way. Players who continued to take a knee this season during pregame ceremonies caused dissension among fans and viewers but also between the players and owners in the league. Many people wanted players who protested while the National Anthem was being performed to not be allowed to play while others believed the owners were blackballing Colin Kaepernick by preventing him from playing quarterback for any NFL team. The action of the owners became more of a distraction than the protests of the players as they made statements that revealed their belief that they owned the team and the players were their property rather than people who they employed to play on their team. It did not help that many of them had supported President Donald Trump who made a disparaging remark about the players.

The revelation that many former NFL players have experienced brain trauma from concussions that has led to CTE is a drawback for the league as more ex-players come forward showing symptoms of CTE and younger players are retiring after playing minimal years in the NFL to avoid the risk of suffering any head collisions that will lead to brain damage. This has become a major concern for many parents who have made the decision to not allow their children to participate in the violent form of the sport as they have seen players in high school and college suffer from concussions and severe spinal injuries. Flag football has become an alternative for those parents who want their children to experience and enjoy playing the sport in a less violent fashion.

In previous seasons, the NFL has had to deal with domestic violence and the abuse of women by its players. A player was caught in the off-season pulling down the top of a woman at a public celebration exposing her breasts. These despicable actions have dulled the image of *"The Shield"* that the league tries to protect at all costs. The NFL has instituted policies on domestic violence and suspended players who have abused women but it still has lost female viewership that consists of mothers who refuse to let their sons play the game. This will cause a problem in the future for high school, college, and NFL team who will have less of a pool to select their players as many boys are being guided toward other sports.

Basketball is a sport that can be played in the driveway, back yard, playground, or gym and the injuries suffered from the game are less severe than in football. The NBA is a sports league in America with players from all over the world and fans far beyond the borders of the States. It has become a global sport by selecting its talents from foreign countries which has grown its fan base vastly and made the players in the league known all over the world. NBA players have become popular from having their names on sneakers and doing advertisement and appearing at basketball camps around the world. Many NBA fans know their favorite players from facial recognition while most NFL fans know their star players from the name on the back of the jersey. Attempts have been made by the NFL to expand the game of football internationally but so far it has been unsuccessful chiefly because many countries already have a sport called football known to Americans as soccer.

On Thanksgiving Day, the NFL is the game that many sports fans watch but on Christmas Day, the NBA is the game that has become the main attraction. A shift is taking place in America for the favorite choice of sport. The NFL became the most popular league after MLB held that position for several generations and now the NBA is going to supplant the NFL as the top sport. It is the game of the youth who are of the same generation as most of the players in the Association and they share similar interests in fashion, music, movies, and social issues. Players are supported when they stand up and speak out for a cause while being considerate to their fans. Not so in the NFL. While many football fans get excited for NCAA football on Saturday, others are losing faith in the Sunday ritual of the NFL. Football is often equated with war and it appears Americans are no longer thrilled with victory while their heroes suffer with CTE and PTSD.

Posted 12/30/2017

SUMMATION.   While the NFL is still popular in America some fans have soured on the league and the games. The response by NFL owners to players kneeling or performing their version of protest during the playing of the National Anthem instead of addressing the issues of the players that has blemished the league and cost it some fans. Nike placed Colin Kaepernick in the lead of their 30th anniversary of the *"Just Do It"* campaign ad and has earned billions of dollars. Kaepernick started the protest in the NFL to bring attention to police brutality and the killing of unarmed Black men. This issue gained significant relevance when Botham Jean was killed by Amber Guyger. Jean was an unarmed Black man in his apartment who was shot by Guyger who is a White police officer and was off-duty at the time after a long shift that she mistook his apartment for her own.

The Carolina Panthers are taking the lead in trying to change their image and improve the view of the league by signing Eric Reid who played and protested with Kaepernick. Carolina is also trying to recover from the workplace misconduct of Jerry Richardson who was forced to sell the team. This was an important issue for women who are also concerned about their sons playing the game and the health of their husbands and boyfriends after they retire from the game. Violence is a major part of the game and the NFL is in the midst of another controversy as it tries to protect the quarterback from injury but their older fans and former players believe it is making the league "*soft.*" This is at a time there is much anticipation for the upcoming NBA season with LeBron James playing for the Los Angeles Lakers and DeMarcus "Boogie" Cousins joining the Golden State Warriors. While the NFL is struggling trying to maintain its core audience and appease current viewers, the NBA is the game with the players the fans want to watch and have the fashion and apparel they want to wear.

Exercises For A Firm Stomach
(3 Ways To Slim Your Waist)

It is that time when people think of all of the foods they have eaten and wishing they would not have had so many drinks because now when they look in the mirror they can see every bite and every sip hanging around their waist. A New Year's resolution is made to correct the situation and to affirm the commitment, a rushed decision to take advantage of a gym membership is signed. Enthusiastic in the beginning as scheduled visits are kept but soon trips to the gym become few and far between however, monthly payments are still being made and that holiday cheer is still hanging around the waist. There is a better experience to shape up the midriff and it can be done at home.

Before starting an exercise program, a visit to the doctor is recommended for a physical examination. Also, it is important to start with an attitude that the weight will not be lost in one day because it was not all gained in one day. A motionless exercise that causes no pain to the back and will tighten stomach muscles is the *plank*. This exercise is similar to a *push-up* but the elbows are used for support instead of the hands. The back is held straight and the stomach muscles will become tense from the gravitational pull to the floor. It can be done for 15, 20, or 30 seconds for 3, 5, or 6 repetitions at the discretion of the beginner doing the exercise. Gradually increase the seconds and repetitions weekly to improve stomach definition. An advance form of this exercise is to alternate bringing a knee to the chest while in the position. This will benefit the lower stomach and overall the exercise will strengthen the posture of the body.

The following exercise will need the use of a *stretch and tone bar*. Lie flat on back with hands on bar on top of stomach and feet on the floor. Bring bar over head keeping arms straight and lift knees to chest at the same time then return to starting position. This exercise is similar to lying on the floor and raising to touch the toes but applies no stress to the back while toning the core of the body. It also provides a great stretch which helps the body be more flexible. For better results, when returning to the starting position keep feet raised off the floor six inches then proceed to the next repetition without feet touching the floor until all repetitions are completed. Advance the exercise by holding the feet off the floor 3-5 seconds before doing the next repetition. This will tone the stomach muscles and results can be seen within a week if done everyday. The *stretch and six inches* is also a great way to tone the legs.

Those annoying *"love handles"* can be difficult to lose but the next exercise will work the oblique muscles and help shed them away. In a seated position holding a dumbbell, weight ball, or weight plate, bend knees and lift feet in the air then turn to one side making the oblique muscles stretch then pause. Turn to the other side and repeat stretch. Return to the starting position and pause before the next repetition. Sets of 15 are the goal but start with a lower number, if necessary. An added step can provide more toning for the stomach and legs. After returning to the starting position, straighten legs and keep feet six inches off the floor then return knees to bended position and proceed with next repetition. While the *sit and twist* exercise will tone the stomach, legs, and oblique muscles, it will also strengthen the back.

Dieting will help trim the stomach but many will become disillusioned when results are not shown on the scale and in the mirror. Eating proper portions of healthy foods, snacking on fruits and nuts, and staying away from very sweet deserts will be more beneficial than a restrictive diet. However, eating excessively means more repetitions and longer workouts will be needed to combat the over indulgence and to remain firm and toned. Doing these 3 exercises daily or every other day for at least 20 minutes can slim the waist and provide a stronger core for the body. There are exercises and equipment that if done and used properly will help people have a firm stomach but unless they have a *"want to"* attitude, they will be making the same resolution for the next year.

Posted 12/31/2017

SUMMATION.   Following a diet high in protein is beneficial in slimming the waist. A high protein diet can help with support health and strength while building lean muscle. It helps to reach the desired goals and contributes in maintaining a strong core and firm midsection after losing weight. A good drink to go along with the diet is alkaline water. It has a higher pH and can neutralize body acid which helps the body fight disease. Alkaline water can reduce symptoms of acid reflux which raises oxygen level and increases energy and metabolism. Some other benefits are aiding in detoxing the body, fights high blood pressure, high cholesterol, and diabetes, strengthens bones, promotes a healthy heart and reduces signs of aging.

Water containing electrolytes are a source of nutrients that are responsible for stimulating muscles and nerves. Sodium, potassium, calcium, magnesium, and phosphate help regulate the amount of fluids throughout the body, which affects cellular function, blood volume and blood pressure. After sweating from a workout, there is a loss of electrolytes. Replenishing the body with electrolyte water can restore the minerals. It is great for preventing dehydration. Drinking plain water is good but it will not replace the essentials as well as electrolyte water. Sport drinks can be beneficial but they must contain no sugars and unnecessary additives. Anything negative put into the body means exercising for a longer period to get it out of the system.